The IEA Health and Welfare Unit

Choice in

Reinventing

The IEA Health and Welfare Unit

Choice in Welfare No. 17

Reinventing Civil Society:
The Rediscovery of Welfare Without Politics

David G. Green

IEA Health and Welfare Unit
London, 1993

First published in 1993
by
The IEA Health and Welfare Unit
2 Lord North St
London SW1P 3LB

© The IEA Health and Welfare Unit 1993

ISBN 0-255 36279-X

Typeset by the IEA Health and Welfare Unit
in Palatino 11 on 12 point
Printed in Great Britain by
Goron Pro-Print Co. Ltd
Churchill Industrial Estate, Lancing, West Sussex

Contents

The Author

Dr David Green is the Director of the Health and Welfare Unit at the Institute of Economic Affairs. He was formerly a Labour councillor in Newcastle upon Tyne from 1976 until 1981, and from 1981 to 1983 was a Research Fellow at the Australian National University in Canberra.

His books include *Power and Party in an English City*, Allen & Unwin, 1980; *Mutual Aid or Welfare State*, Allen & Unwin, 1984, with L. Cromwell; *Working Class Patients and the Medical Establishment*, Temple Smith/Gower, 1985; and *The New Right: The Counter Revolution in Political, Economic and Social Thought*, Wheatsheaf, 1987. His work has also been published in journals such as *The Journal of Social Policy, Political Quarterly, Philosophy of the Social Sciences* and *Policy and Politics*.

The IEA has published his *The Welfare State: For Rich or for Poor*, 1982; *Which Doctor?*, 1985; *Challenge to the NHS*, 1986; *Medicines in the Marketplace*, 1987; *Everyone a Private Patient*, 1988; *Should Doctors Advertise?*, 1989; *Equalizing People*, 1990; and (with David Lucas) *Medicard: A Better Way to Pay for Medicines?*, 1993.

Acknowledgements

This book reflects ten years of continuing conversation with Arthur
Seldon and Ralph Harris from which I have been the chief beneficiary. Arthur Seldon's support and encouragement over many years has
been valuable beyond measure and Ralph Harris made especially
useful detailed comments which improved the final version substantially. My thanks also go to IEA colleagues John Blundell and Colin
Robinson for useful criticisms of an early draft.

I have benefited from research assistance provided by David
Lucas, assistant director of the IEA Health and Welfare Unit, and Gur
Hirshberg, who was an intern at the IEA in the summer of 1993. I
have also received excellent advice from several members of the
Advisory Council of the IEA Health and Welfare Unit, particularly
Peter Saunders, Bob Pinker, Tom Griffin, George Teeling-Smith, Jon
Davies, Michael Beesley, Norman Barry, Peter Collison, Sir Reginald
Murley and Max Hartwell. I feel very fortunate to be able to rely on
receiving such high-quality advice. My thanks also go to Tom Palmer
of the Institute for Humane Studies, whose request to prepare a paper
for the Eastern Europe Outreach Programme prompted me to write
this book and who offered valuable criticisms of a much earlier
version.

Two friends, Norman Dennis and Michael Novak deserve a
special mention for their help. I have profited greatly from many
hours of discussion with Norman Dennis stretching over 20 years,
and usually in the congenial surroundings of the beautiful hills of
England. Michael Novak has become a frequent visitor to the IEA
during the last four years. He has taught me a great deal, and I am
especially grateful to him for suggesting several invaluable improvements to *Reinventing Civil Society* during his most recent visit as
Wincott Visiting Fellow. It goes without saying that the remaining
errors, oversights and omissions are my responsibility.

Finally, may I record sincere thanks to the Esmée Fairbairn
Charitable Trust for its generous support of the three-year programme
of research and study which made possible the production of this
book.

David Green

Preface

This book began as an attempt to consider the lessons the former communist countries of Eastern Europe might be able to learn from Western experience of voluntary welfare provision. But, as the study proceeded, it quickly became obvious that we in the West have done almost as much harm to our own voluntary associations as the communist countries, not as part of a deliberate effort to create a mass society of individuals ruled by an elite, but as a result of the inadvertent displacement effect of the welfare state. By narrowing opportunities for personal idealism in the service of others, the welfare state has eroded the sense of personal responsibility and mutual obligation on which a resilient civil society rests.

As I began to think about how best we could re-invigorate our once rich and varied voluntary, communal life it also became obvious that the economic philosophy which had come to dominance in the 1980s did not provide intellectual tools adequate to the task. This inadequacy was particulary reflected in the social policies of the Thatcher years, which were dominated by a hard-boiled economic rationalism which failed to do justice to human character and potential.

We only have to look at our own language to discover the rich variety of virtues that make a free society work and which describe the obligations we all owe to one another. Good character, honesty, duty, self-sacrifice, honour, service, self-discipline, toleration, respect, justice, self-improvement, trust, civility, fortitude, courage, integrity, diligence, patriotism, consideration for others, thrift and reverence are just a few. Yet many of these words cannot readily be used today in ordinary talk. To the modern ear, they have a ring of either antique charm or total obsolescence.

The leading voices of Thatcherite philosophy invariably saw the Thatcher revolution in moral terms. They hoped to restore what Shirley Letwin, in her excellent book *The Anatomy of Thatcherism*, called the 'vigorous virtues' of self-sufficiency, energy, independent mindedness, adventurousness, loyalty to friends and hardiness in the face of enemies.[1] The Thatcherite emphasis on the vigorous virtues was of central importance in halting the pace of Britain's genteel economic decline. And today, the superiority of robust market competition compared with socialist planning is accepted across the political spectrum. But, Thatcherism suffered from a missing ingredient. It is the thesis of this book that the missing dimension was its inadequate emphasis on the 'civic virtues', such as self-sacrifice, duty, solidarity and service of others.

Over twenty years ago in 1971 the IEA's Editorial Director, Arthur Seldon, commissioned *The Morals of Markets*[2] by the philosopher H.B. Acton to examine the moral questions raised by competition. In the heat of the subsequent battle to improve public understanding of economic problems, the issues raised in that book were put to one side but now, in recognition of its continuing relevance, the Liberty Fund has republished *The Morals of Markets*. *Reinventing Civil Society* is an attempt to refine and develop further our thinking about the moral dimension of a free society.

David G. Green

Introduction

During the Thatcher years there were many who feared that the welfare state would be 'dismantled'. In fact, the welfare state remained almost unscathed because the most radical reforms attempted by Thatcher administrations did not even aspire to 'dismantle' the welfare state. Thatcher Governments often used market rhetoric, such as 'money following the patient's choice' or 'money following the parents' choice of school', but in reality ministers were working with a very restricted idea of the market. The NHS reforms, for instance, led to an 'internal market' not all that different from any other government procurement programme. Thatcher Governments also worked with too narrow a view of human character. The education reforms, for example, were based on a consumerist view of parents as outsiders standing in judgement of schools, rather than as co-partners in the long process of equipping their own children with the skills, knowledge and personal qualities necessary in a free, open and tolerant society.

Economic rationalism dominated the 1980s primarily because we had come through a period in which the battle of ideas had been fought between two economic systems, capitalism and socialism. The conflict between collectivist economic planning and dispersed commercial decision-making in competitive markets inevitably dominated post-war debate because the world was divided into two blocs, communist and capitalist. And the ideology defending communism, as well as milder forms of collectivism, insisted that the economic base determined the social order. Opponents of collectivism had little option, therefore, but to concentrate their attack on communist economics. But in drawing attention to the merits of markets, some advocates of freedom lost sight of the historic ideal which in reality made Western civilisation superior to communism.

With the benefit of hindsight, we can now see that this preoccupation with economics diverted our gaze from the deeper questions facing any civilisation. Markets generate more prosperity, but 'more goods' do not make a good society and its capacity to create 'more goods' is not alone what makes capitalism superior to communism.

What then was the historic ideal of liberty? Most people would describe Britain loosely as a free society, but when we speak of freedom what precisely do we have in mind? Today's challenge is no longer to show the superiority of markets over central planning, but to deepen understanding of that complex of institutions which makes possible, not only prosperity, but rather progress in all spheres of human existence, whether in art, education, welfare, morals, religion, community service, neighbourly help, or anything else; and, no less important, which allows for human diversity without endangering freedom and the safety of the streets.

As Adam Smith recognised, it is possible for a society to hang together if it is based only on mutual advantage. Self-interest does not always mean selfishness; there is much scope for harmonious agreement; and people with selfish intentions will find that the discipline of competition tends to channel their energies into serving others. However, as Adam Smith also acknowledged in *The Theory of Moral Sentiments*, such claims only take us so far and for Smith and other early pioneers of classical liberalism, people ought to be guided in their lives not only by self interest but also by duty, indeed in Smith's view 'Christian duty'.

The freedom celebrated by Smith was not only a theory accounting pragmatically for social cohesion amidst self-interest, it was also an ideal which challenged every person to discover his or her better self. As Michael Novak has written, a free society 'demands much of individuals, because it expects them to be free. The source of a nation's beauty, and of the love its citizens bear it, is that it asks so much of them'.[1]

The thinkers who dominated public policy making in the 1980s did not conceive liberty in these terms. They were inclined to adopt what Frank Knight, the doyen of the Chicago school of economists, called a 'hard-boiled pose', abhorring all such talk of ideals or virtues or high motives as sentimentality.[2] This group of hard-boiled economic rationalists was often positively hostile to any talk of 'social responsibility' or 'moral obligation'. They had good reason for their suspicion, because socialists have frequently disguised their efforts to grab political power behind a smokescreen of talk about 'social' responsibility, by which they meant 'political' action. But 'social' does not inevitably mean 'political'. There is much common activity which is not political and one of the chief measures of the quality of a free civilisation is the richness of its voluntary, communal life.

Hard-boiled suspicion of political controversy couched in moral terms was also not wholly misplaced, again because socialists have not seen the good person as someone who gave his own time and energy in the service of others, but as the individual who demanded action by the state at the expense of other taxpayers. This politicised interpretation of moral responsibility, far from increasing consideration for others, tends to undermine the sense of personal responsibility on which an ethos of service truly rests. But not everyone professing a moral view is a closet socialist, and the challenge we face today is to identify a sense of community or solidarity that is compatible with freedom. Competitive markets coordinate the efforts of people who may be self-interested, even selfish, but they do not create solidarity. Contrary to the view attributed to Mrs Thatcher, that there is 'no such thing as society', there is indeed such a thing. But it is not synonymous with the state. It is the realm of 'activity in common', which is at once voluntary and guided by a sense of duty to other people and to the social system on which liberty rests.[3] The hard-boiled economic rationalists have tended to be satisfied with the coordinating effect of market competition, but as Adam Smith recognised, the good society requires more than coordination. Liberty rests on people taking personal responsibility for the maintenance of the institutions, morals and habits fundamental to freedom.

This tradition of 'communal liberalism' is not a utopian ideal of the imagination, it was the lived reality of liberty for many long years until well into the twentieth century. Most of this book is an attempt to describe the day-to-day character of this tradition by re-assessing the voluntary social institutions that had emerged under its influence by the end of the last century, when their incomplete evolution was prematurely halted by the march of socialism. To understand the character of an historical movement we must turn, not only to the writings of its intellectual leaders, but also to the conduct of the humbler citizens of the land. For liberty was not only an intellectual ideal, it was the guiding philosophy of the common people who acted out its values in their everyday lives. This reality is nowhere better exemplified than in the work of the friendly societies, those organisations for mutual aid which flourished in the eighteenth, nineteenth and early twentieth centuries and which were joined by the vast majority of working men, far exceeding the membership of the other characteristic organisations of the working classes, the trade unions and the co-operative societies. (In 1910 there were 6.6m registered members of friendly societies; 2.5m members of registered trade unions; and 2.5m members of co-operative societies.)[4]

The friendly societies are of additional interest for two other reasons. First, the record of the friendly societies contradicts the wide perception today that, although a market society is undoubtedly the best way to generate prosperity, it provides inadequately for the health and welfare of its citizens. As Chapters 3-10 relate, the historical reality turns out to have been the opposite of the legend of welfare before the welfare state widely believed today.

And second, the experience of the friendly societies shows that we have under-estimated the displacement effect of the welfare state. Thatcher Governments thought it an adequate response to defects in the health service, for example, to introduce competitive tendering within the state system. But this was to misunderstand the true character of a free society. Competitive markets are a necessary but not sufficient condition of freedom. The welfare state did not only suppress the incentive system of the competitive market, it also suppressed those institutions which served as proving grounds for men and women of good character and which provided outlets for idealism, service and achievement. We must therefore find new ways to re-energise 'civil society'. The final chapter proposes how this renewal might be accomplished.

Partly for want of a convenient label and partly to contrast it with the tradition I have been calling hard-boiled economic rationalism, I will dub the collection of maxims, guiding principles, beliefs and dispositions which I am recommending 'civic capitalism'.[5] The term is intended to imply support for competitive markets in economic affairs, combined with a recognition that a free society worthy of the name also rests on civic duty, that is on an ethos of shared personal responsibility for the well-being of our fellows. The challenge is to foster and maintain this ethos of mutual respect with the minimum resort to political action, a realm which today is grievously distorted by the shallow factionalism of modern party politics.

1

The Institutions Fundamental to Liberty

This chapter describes the problems with which the founders of civic capitalism were concerned, focusing on their underlying assumptions about the human condition and the key institutions to which they attached importance.

It does not seek to describe every school of thought which has been called liberal at one time or another, but rather to trace a particular tradition of liberal thought which has been described as well by Michael Oakeshott as by anyone. It rests not on any one idea, but on a complex of interlocking institutions and individual dispositions. These include antipathy to overwhelming concentrations of power, whether in the hands of the state or any other organisation; support for a democratic but limited form of government, in part to check over-mighty rulers but also out of respect for the dignity of the individual; and a strong sense of social solidarity built upon the recognition that the social system depends on every person doing their bit to maintain a climate of mutual regard and consideration for others by accepting the moral obligations which derive from the Judeo-Christian tradition. Its roots can be traced back at least to the thirteenth century, but as a modern tradition it can be discovered in the work of Locke in the seventeenth century, through Smith in the eighteenth, Acton and Tocqueville in the nineteenth, and Oakeshott, Hayek and Michael Novak in the twentieth.

The Essence of Liberty

As Michael Oakeshott has observed, a person declares his support for liberty not because he begins with an abstract definition of liberty which he then compares with the real world, as an engineer compares a piece of metal with a template. Rather, it is because he has found a particular way of living to be good. The purpose of inquiry into liberty, therefore, is not to define a word, but 'to detect the secret of what we enjoy, to recognise what is hostile to it, and to discern where and how it may be enjoyed more fully'.[1] This too was F.A. Hayek's approach. He did not set out to define freedom, but to understand what was valuable about the freedom that had been enjoyed by Western nations.

What, then, have been the characteristics of Britain which made it free? First, if Oakeshott is correct, we cannot draw up a list of the institutions which comprise liberty. Liberties can be distinguished, but the freedom known to our forbears rested, not on separate rights, laws or institutions, but on many mutually supporting liberties:

> it springs neither from the separation of church and state, nor from the rule of law, nor from private property, nor from parliamentary government, nor from the writ of *habeas corpus*, nor from the independence of the judiciary, nor from any one of the thousand other devices and arrangements and characteristics of our society, but from what each signifies and represents, namely, the absence from our society of overwhelming concentrations of power.

This absence of concentrations of power is, according to Oakeshott, the general characteristic of freedom which subsumes the others. First, authority is divided between the past, the present and the future:

> we should consider a society governed wholly by its past, or its present, or its future to suffer under a despotism of superstition which forbids freedom. The politics of our society are a conversation in which past, present and future each has a voice; and though one or other of them may on occasion prevail, none permanently dominates, and on this account we are free.[2]

Second, power is dispersed among the organisations and interests which comprise society:

> We do not fear or seek to suppress diversity of interest, but we consider our freedom to be imperfect so long as the dispersal of power among them is incomplete, and to be threatened if any one interest or combination of interests, even though it may be the interest of the majority, acquires extraordinary power.[3]

In essence, then, we consider ourselves free because: 'no one in our society is allowed unlimited power—no leader, faction, party or "class", no majority, no government, church, corporation, trade or professional association or trade union'. The secret of our freedom is that our society 'is composed of a multitude of organisations in the constitution of the best of which is reproduced that diffusion of power which is characteristic of the whole'.[4] The friendly societies, and especially the affiliated orders which are described in Chapters 3-7, were just such organisations.

The Legacy of the Middle Ages

If Oakeshott is correct in identifying the absence of overwhelming concentrations of power as the essence of liberty, how can we account for the peculiar character of the state in Britain? According to Oakeshott, modern European states can best be understood as torn between two contradictory methods of association which are the legacy of the medieval age. The first mode of association he calls 'civil association' and the second 'enterprise' or 'purposive association'.

An 'enterprise association' is composed of persons related in the pursuit of a common interest or objective. In the pure form of such an association there are not several purposes, but one sovereign purpose. The task of leaders is to manage the pursuit of this goal and to direct individuals as appropriate. A nation might comprise many such enterprise associations, including business corporations, but here I am concerned with nation-states which take on this character.

In a nation of civil associates people are related to one another, not because they share a concrete goal, or are engaged together in a substantive task, but in that they acknowledge the authority of the jurisdiction under which they live. Respect for the authority of the law does not imply that every person supports every law. The law is a changing phenomenon, and so what commands respect in a civil association is both the law as it stands and the law-reforming process.

The laws specify the conditions to which every person subscribes as each pursues his or her self-chosen life style. This type of association is therefore a system of law and its jurisdiction. People are associated, not because they share the same substantive wants, but because they accept the same conditions in seeking to pursue their own goals as they believe best.[5] Each is under an obligation to act justly towards others, and each person enjoys equal status under the jurisdiction. The character of the laws is central. In both an enterprise association and a civil association people are subject to rules of conduct, but in an enterprise association the rules are instrumental to the pursuit of the common aim. In the pure form of civil association, the laws are moral stipulations, not instrumental commands.[6]

Under a system of civil association the sense of solidarity of the people as well as the legitimacy of the government derives from the shared sense that the social system gives everyone their chance to do the best they can in their self-chosen sphere of life and also from popular awareness that the continuance of liberty depends on everyone doing their bit. The sense of solidarity in an enterprise association, however, derives from the belief that each person is part of a single grand scheme, in practice either to modernise or develop the nation's resources or to mould human character in a new direction. Thus, in a nation organised as an enterprise association, individuals are instruments of the government; whereas in a civil association the government is an instrument of the people, charged with keeping in good order the institutions which allow people to pursue their self-chosen ideals.

Historically, Oakeshott characterises the two types of association as outcomes of medieval thought and practice. The enterprise association approximates to 'lordship' and the civil association to 'rulership'. In medieval times kings were lords of their domain or estate, and therefore managers of their people. Kingship in the age of lordship was, therefore, estate management. The King was lord of the manor.

According to Oakeshott, on the Continent by the fifteenth century the lords of the emerging realms of the time were evolving into rulers.[7] As a ruler, the king was custodian of the laws and enforcer of justice and the subjects of such a ruler were free to go about their lives without intrusion so long as they obeyed the laws. In Britain, emerging rulership had been noticed in the thirteenth century by writers such as Henry Bracton, the judge and chancellor of Exeter Cathedral who compiled the first systematic account of English laws and customs. On the continent, the realms Oakeshott had in mind were Austria, Brandenburg-Prussia, Bavaria, Saxony, Wurttemburg, and Westphalia, whose rulers had graduated from being lords of tenants and territories to being kings of sovereign realms and subjects.[8] These emerging realms were no longer landed estates, nor were they merely military alliances, rather they were legal associations. The emergent ruler was:

> neither a *grand seigneur*, the lordly proprietor of a domain, nor the leader of a host, nor one concerned to exercise an undefined moral and prudential guardianship over the lives, the activities, and the fortunes of his people; he was a ruler of subjects ... whose office was to perform certain public duties, distinguished (though with some difficulty) from his private concerns.[9]

The state as bequeathed to modern European nations by history may be understood as an unresolved tension between these two irreconcilable dispositions, lordship (enterprise association) and rulership (civil association).

In the twentieth century we can recognise totalitarianism as the modern parallel of enterprise association and classical liberalism as the counterpart of civil association. In Oakeshott's terminology we can understand the development of Western democracies in the twentieth century, and especially Britain, as a steady evolution from civil association to enterprise association. For the classical liberal, civil association is the more desirable of the two, but there is no implication that enterprise association is always bad. It is possible for a civil association to transform itself temporarily into an enterprise association, as the Western democracies did during World War Two.

The Practical Problems that Concerned Seventeenth Century Liberals

In England modern liberalism emerged as the ruling philosophy during the seventeenth-century struggle between the crown and parliament.[10] The defenders of liberty took the line that, in asserting the divine right of kings, the Stuart monarchs were departing from the tradition of liberty under law which had been the birthright of the English since at least the thirteenth century. The English subject, the parliamentarians reasoned, was entitled to be ruled by laws, not the whims of any king.

Similar ideas crossed the Atlantic to America where they inspired the war of independence and the American constitution. And comparable movements evolved in Germany and France in opposition to the absolutist rulers of those countries.

In the seventeenth century the power of the state, in the form of the king and the established church, was seen as an obstacle to the self-directing person. Liberalism originated as a reaction to this state of affairs, seeking release from the fetters constraining economic life, religion, politics and intellectual affairs. Liberals wanted an end to religious persecution and sought freedom of conscience, thought and expression. Many went further still, demanding no enforced interpreter between man and the Scriptures and no intermediary between man and God. Some chose to elect their priests by a free vote of church members.

Liberals sought security from criminals and looked to the state to provide it. But because they were keenly aware that the state's protective role could be abused, they wanted its powers to be severely circumscribed. Consequently they sought equality before the law and the independence of the judicial tribunals from the legislative and executive arms of government. They wanted complete freedom of movement from place to place and job to job, to enable individuals or families to find their own niche. They sought the freedom to exchange products and services at mutually agreed prices, to accumulate capital and to lend and borrow freely. They wanted everyone to enjoy the right to own and use property as each thought best. And they sought to end the king's habit of granting royal monopolies to favoured groups in return for payment. In 1621, according to one estimate, there were about 700 royal monopolies forcing up the prices of many common household goods such as candles, coal, soap, leather, salt and pepper.[11] The liberal remedy was to demand that the king must not make laws to benefit (or disadvantage) particular, known individuals or groups.

If Lord Acton was correct, the desire for freedom of worship was the dominant factor in the emergence of liberalism. It was, he said, the 'deepest current' in 1641 and the 'strongest motive' in 1688. Men learnt that it was only by abridging the power of governments that the liberty of churches could be assured. That great political idea, wrote Acton:

> sanctifying freedom and consecrating it to God, teaching men to treasure the liberties of others as their own, and to defend them for love of justice and charity more than as a claim of right, has been the soul of what is great and good in the progress of the last two hundred years.[12]

This seventeenth-century antipathy to over-mighty government developed in two directions, not always clearly distinguished. The first, which I will call civic capitalism in the hope of avoiding confusion with other related ideas, can be understood as an effort to prevent the king from reverting to 'lordship', in Oakeshott's language. The civic capitalist ideal was a nation united as civil associates, not as instruments of the king's will. This antipathy to the king was based on a sense, entrenched since at least the thirteenth century, that English subjects were governed by a ruler not by a lord, and that the law was a moral and prudential code for living which no person, and certainly no king, ought to defy. The Stuart kings were seen as usurpers meddling with the centuries-old rights of subjects. Classical liberalism, or civic capitalism, was therefore respectful of history. It saw England's civilisation as worth preserving.

The other leading liberal tradition is commonly called rationalism. It did not see the struggle against the Stuart monarchs as a restoration of historic rights, but rather saw all tradition as suffocating, and barely distinguished between custom and superstition. This tradition originated with Descartes and, in its search for 'clear and distinct' truth, over-estimated the capacity of governments to re-arrange human affairs. Spokesmen for the classical-liberal tradition, such as Locke, were more modest in their claims:

> Since ... it is unavoidable to the greatest part of men, if not all, to have several *opinions*, without certain and indubitable proofs of their truths; it would, methinks, become all men to maintain peace and the common offices of humanity and friendship in the diversity of opinions. We should do well to commiserate our mutual ignorance, and endeavour to remove it in all the gentle and fair ways of information; and not instantly treat others ill, as obstinate and perverse, because they will not renounce their own, and receive our opinions.[13]

Rationalistic liberals were confident that they were right and self-assertive in pursuing their goals. In the hands of such men this brand of liberalism stimulated the tendency of Western politics to revert to lordship, that is, the central direction of people and property.

The Civic Capitalist's Underlying Assumptions About the Human Condition

How did the civic capitalists see the human condition? Essentially, they saw it as a struggle against human imperfection. Two particular shortcomings concerned them, sinfulness and ignorance, and consequently the practical task of the civic-capitalist thinker and activist was to develop human civilisation by discovering or improving those institutions which encouraged the opposites of sin and ignorance, namely goodness and learning. The moral ideal underlying civic capitalism is that human relations should, as far as possible, be based on free mutual consent rather than force or command. Classical liberals favoured this ideal because they believed it was more consistent with human nature than rule by the 'lord of the manor'. But it was also an ideal in the sense that it challenged human character by setting a standard to be aimed for. It presented people with an ideal way to live.

The particular combination of institutions that came to be supported had taken reasonably mature shape by the time that liberals like David Hume, Adam Smith, Josiah Tucker, Edmund Burke and William Paley were writing in the eighteenth century. The character of civic capitalism was elaborated further during the American constitutional debates of the 1780s, not least by the authors of the *Federalist Papers*, by Immanuel Kant and Wilhelm von Humboldt in Germany, by Montesquieu in France and during the nineteenth century by Tocqueville, J.S. Mill and Acton. During this century the tradition has been developed still further by Friedrich Hayek and Michael Novak.[14]

It is important to avoid one major source of modern confusion. Liberty under law is not a doctrine which sees liberty as the absence of all restraint, or freedom from all obstacles to our desires. The classical liberals did not want 'power', they wanted 'liberty', that is they did not seek the 'power' to achieve their particular ambitions, they sought a social order—a civilisation—which allowed every person the liberty under law to contribute to their own good and the good of others as each believed best. To repeat Acton's words: they treasured the liberties of others as their own.

The ideal was liberty under law, not liberty to do as anyone pleased.[15] It was liberty guided by conscience rather than naked wants. Nor was it relativistic. Liberty was valued, not because civic capitalists thought that any individual's views or values were as good as anyone else's, but because it is not possible for any authority to identify in advance who will turn out to do the most good, or benefit humankind to the greatest extent, or to judge which values, habits or institutions will ultimately prove most conducive to human co-operation. Consequently, they thought that every one should be free to contribute as each thought proper, in the belief that we will recognise real progress when we see it.

The view of thinkers such as Acton and Tocqueville must also be sharply distinguished from another attitude often associated with liberalism. It is the view, which derives from Rousseau, that people are essentially good and that they are made bad by institutions, such as bad laws or bad governments. From this belief it follows that, if we wish to perfect human beings, we must first eradicate the institutions which corrupt them. Such thinking was a powerful influence on the French revolutionaries, who discovered to their cost that if you eradicate a nation's traditions and institutions then each citizen ends by facing alone one organised power, the army. For the civic capitalists, people were not inherently good. Life was a constant struggle against imperfection, in which the social system played a vital part along with individual conscience.

Closely linked to the idea of the 'noble savage' was another belief which also originated in France. The thinkers of the French Enlightenment of the second half of the eighteenth century took the view that nature was knowable through the senses, from which they concluded that all other interpretations were wrong. Consequently they put great faith in scientific knowledge and were inclined to reject all church teaching as mere superstition. Voltaire, for instance, despised the clergy, as did Condorcet, who believed that when kings, aristocrats and priests had been swept aside then men would be free and equal. (Rousseau was a devout believer in God and did not share the antipathy of the *philosophes* to religion.)

Having disposed of Christianity as superstition, the *philosophes* found it necessary to account for morality. They concluded that, since its source could not be God's commandments, it must be the mutual need of men for one another. All moral rules were seen as sacrifices for the sake of convenience, or in the extreme form of this argument put by Helvetius, all morality was reduced to the calculation of mutual advantage.

This line of thinking found its way to England via William Godwin, Thomas Paine and Jeremy Bentham. Godwin expected the natural harmony of human life to lead to the end of government. Paine wanted to make a clean sweep of kings, aristocrats, priests and their superstitions, and to start again with the rights of man. And Bentham put his trust in the improvement of human life by means of law reform, and saw individuals as rational calculators of their own advantages. The classical economists fell under the influence of David Ricardo,[16] who disregarded the careful teachings of Adam Smith in *The Theory of Moral Sentiments*, and studied human behaviour as if people were economic rationalists or pleasure seekers out to maximise their own gain. Self-sacrifice and duty, if they were entertained at all, were seen as no different from any other human satisfaction.

The Moral and Legal Foundations of Freedom

What civic capitalists sought was a complex of institutions which, on the one hand, minimised the harm that bad people might do, and on the other, left room for the best in people to flourish and grow.

The vital foundation for a society which allowed room for initiative and change was seen as the moral order, often reinforced by praise or blame varying in intensity from ostracism to the raised eyebrow, but also by threats of punishment in well-recognised cases. The law in the strict sense is those moral rules enforced by threats of punishment. The idea of the 'rule of law' is rather wider. To civic capitalists it meant government by laws not men.

The rule of law is partly a theory of government which holds that government should be under the law and that the legislature should be separate from the executive as well as from the judges. It is also a theory about the appropriate character of law. Legislators should make laws of a particular type only, above all, laws should be general and not serve particular interests. This idea was more readily understood in earlier centuries than it is today. In the seventeenth century a distinction was commonly made between laws and proclamations.[17] Laws were permanent rules which outlived any individual; proclamations lasted only during the king's lifetime and were orders to his servants to carry out particular tasks. Hayek later captured this distinction by differentiating between 'rules of just conduct' and 'commands'.

The law was valuable for two reasons, first it deterred bad people from harming others, and second it created a stable environment in which people could use their own knowledge and skills as they believed best because they could count on the enforcement of known rules.

The civic-capitalist view of human knowledge was that individuals knew more about their own circumstances than any government official. Burke expressed the idea clearly in *Reflections on the Revolution in France*:

> in my course I have known, and, according to my measure, have co-operated with great men; and I have never yet seen any plan which has not been mended by the observations of those who were much inferior in understanding to the person who took the lead in the business.[18]

As Hayek later explained, so much of the knowledge and skill that is useful to us is carried by individuals, either consciously or as unconscious habit, and consequently a society would tend to be prosperous if it allowed individuals to make the best use of the knowledge which only they possessed. Liberty under law provided the circumstances which made possible this freedom of initiative.

Laws and Prosperity

According to Adam Smith, without law human energy tended to be wasted amidst criminality. In his view, the prosperity of England was the outcome of its laws, a situation which he contrasted with some Eastern countries where possessions could be taken at will by the ruler. Consequently, in such countries people tended to bury coins and valuable objects to hide them from marauding kings and emperors. In response, it became established in many countries that buried treasure was the property of the monarch. Treasure trove, as buried treasure became known, was acquired on a sufficient scale in some countries to be a significant part of the ruler's income. The laws of England gave people security of person and property:

> In the midst of all the exactions of government ... capital has been silently and gradually accumulated by the private frugality and good conduct of individuals, by their universal, continual, and uninterrupted effort to better their own condition. It is this effort, protected by law and allowed by liberty to exert itself in the manner that is most advantageous, which has maintained the progress of England towards opulence and improvement in almost all former times.[19]

The law is intended, not only to punish wrong conduct, but also to smooth the path of voluntary co-operation. Roughly speaking, criminal law punishes moral wrongs, and civil law is the body of rules that makes it easier to work with other people, as buyers or sellers, employers or employees, and consequently to create wealth more readily.

Thus, civic capitalism was a political philosophy based on a belief in the possibility (but not the inevitability) of progress and how it could best be achieved. In essence, civic capitalists have taken the view that progress is the result of trial and error. As the distinguished turn-of-the-century economist Alfred Marshall argued, collectivism might seem in the short run to deliver benefits, but this was only because it lived off the fruits of earlier private initiative. In Marshall's view, if the springs of progress were not to dry up, there was no substitute for the bearing of risks at one's own expense.[20]

The Character of Liberal Law

Recognition that law was necessary for prosperity brought in its train the risk that the power of punishment might be abused. The remedy of the classical liberals was to confine all punishment to the state, and

16

further to require the state to threaten punishment by one means alone, namely in the form of laws which were declared in advance and which set out principles of right conduct. This concept of law also requires a little elaboration because it differs from the twentieth-century view. Since the Middle Ages, and certainly since the thirteenth century law had not been seen as 'any properly carried resolution of parliament', it was understood to be 'already there' waiting to be discovered by scholars and judges. Judges *found* laws or *declared* them, they did not *make* them. In part, the law was seen as God's province, not a realm open to interference by mere mortals. It was also seen as embodying the wisdom of generations, for when Adam Smith was writing in the eighteenth century most law was common law, not deliberately-enacted legislation.

Indeed, until the nineteenth century there was relatively little deliberately-made law. Later, towards the end of the nineteenth century and especially during the twentieth, it became acceptable for governments to make whatever laws they liked and the idea of government under the law lost its meaning. Today, law is the chief instrument of government in the achievement of its policy goals. The executive has, in effect, captured the legislature. The politicisation of law-making was given added momentum at the end of the nineteenth century when new voters came on to the electoral register. Political parties vied for the support of the new working-class voters by enacting legislation to buy their votes, a tendency of special relevance to the voluntary sector to be discussed later.

In Oakeshott's terminology, Britain reverted to an older style of government, 'enterprise association' rather than 'civil association'. No government in British history has ever been a pure civil association or a pure enterprise association. There has been continuing tension, but in the years after World War Two the pendulum swung decisively in the direction of enterprise association. But Britain never took on the character of the most extreme type, communism, which would not tolerate actions inconsistent with its sovereign aim, nor organisations with separate purposes. Under such regimes, persons are, in effect, the property of the state, so that, where they work or live or whether they leave altogether is a management decision. The 'freedom' of people in such an association is: 'the condition of being released from every care in the world save one; namely, the care not to be idle in fulfilling one's role in the enterprise, not to inhibit or prejudice that complete mobilisation of resources which constitutes such a state'.[21]

17

Social systems of this type, says Oakeshott, replace the seeking of elusive satisfactions and the attendant risk of failure, with assured benefits.[22]

To summarise: for civic capitalists human wrongdoing meant that there must be threats of punishment. But human sinfulness also meant that the agency of punishment, the state, must be limited, lest its powers be abused. People should be ruled by laws not men, meaning that they should be ruled by established rules of right behaviour, not the preferences of the monarch or the majority in parliament.

The main danger to avoid was that the state would become the instrument of narrow private purposes. In seventeenth and eighteenth century England, there was wide acceptance of the importance of the impartiality of government. Different religions had in their turn experienced persecution; Royalists had persecuted their opponents; then Cromwell had turned the tables on them; and after the Restoration the Royalists got their own back.[23] The result was that all the powerful groups came to see the value of denying the power of the state to *all* vested interests including themselves. It meant each group must give up hope of capturing the state for its own purposes, so long as all other powerful groups made a similar sacrifice.

The Rule of law and the Scope of the State

Civic capitalists saw two roles for government. The first was to uphold justice, and in that role they believed that the power of the government ought to be severely curtailed to prevent abuse. Hence the idea of rule by laws, not men. The second function was to provide services paid for by taxes. Here the limiting condition was the necessity for the government to secure the consent of the majority of the people who were to be taxed.

Some liberals, such as Herbert Spencer, took the view that the state should be confined to enforcing and maintaining the criminal law:

> What, then, do they want a government for? Not to regulate commerce; not to educate the people; not to teach religion; not to administer charity; not to make roads and railways; but simply to defend the natural rights of man—to protect person and property—to prevent the aggressions of the powerful upon the weak—in a word to administer justice. This is the natural, the original, office of a government. It was not intended to do less; it ought not to be allowed to do more.[24]

Other classical liberals drew a clear distinction between the state as upholder of justice and the state as servant of the people. This distinction is inherent in the work of Smith and his contemporaries, but was not made fully explicit until J.S. Mill was writing in the nineteenth century (below p. 124). Civic-capitalist mistrust of government was not directed against all government actions *per se*, but against those which reduced the scope for trial and error by monopolising the means of achieving desired ends. I will discuss how this approach might be applied in practice in the concluding chapter, and here only set out the general principles.

Hayek stressed repeatedly that the problem of defining the limit of coercion 'is not the same as that concerning the proper function of government'. The coercive activities of government are by no means its only tasks.[25] Lest there be any doubt about his view, Hayek warns against *laissez-faire*:

> Not Locke, nor Hume, nor Smith, nor Burke, could ever have argued, as Bentham did, that "every law is an evil for every law is an infraction of liberty". Their argument was never a complete *laissez-faire* argument ... They knew better than most of their later critics that it was not some sort of magic but the evolution of "well-constructed institutions" ... that had successfully channelled individual efforts to socially beneficial aims. In fact, their argument was never anti-state as such, or anarchistic, which is the logical outcome of the rationalistic *laissez-faire* doctrine; it was an argument that accounted both for the proper functions of the state and for the limits of state action.[26]

If liberty is not infringed, that is, if the state continues to treat people as civil associates, then whether or not the government should provide a service depends on practical questions such as whether the cost, including any hidden costs, exceeds any benefit. Moreover, even when government action is justified it should not necessarily provide a service itself but rather finance it by hiring competitive private agencies. Reasonable people could easily disagree about the balance of cost and advantage between public and private provision or direct supply compared with competitive tendering, and since there is no absolute right answer, trial and error provides the best remedy. Hence Hayek thought that there was much to be said for competition between a variety of local jurisdictions:

> The range and variety of government action that is, at least in principle, reconcilable with a free system is thus considerable. The old formulae of

laissez-faire or non-intervention do not provide us with an adequate criterion for distinguishing between what is and what is not admissible in a free system. There is ample scope for experimentation and improvement within that permanent legal framework which makes it possible for a free society to operate most efficiently.[27]

If Hayek is right, then part of the answer may lie in creating institutions which allow wide experimentation with different styles of government. In other words the remedy may be a competitive market in regulatory styles achieved by leaving as little as possible to central government, and as much as possible to localities, financed by local taxes with free movement of people, goods and money to allow wide experimentation with the risks of over- and under-government. My distinguished colleague, Arthur Seldon, has argued that we should learn to take the risks of under-government. A decentralised system would allow some localities to be run by those willing to take the risks of under-government and *vice versa*. Such competition in styles of government would allow each locality to learn from the successes and failures of others.

However, the chief drawback of 'taxation by consent' as a limiting principle of government has been that democracy in the twentieth century has come to mean that the power of the majority ought to be unlimited. Moreover, a further damaging development, not fully understood until Hayek described it, was that the unlimited power of the majority came to apply not only to the power to raise taxes, but also to law-making itself, with the result that the very means of limiting the power of government—the law—was politicised and captured by governments. The West has yet to overcome this problem.

2

The Indispensable Ethos of Liberty: Personal Responsibility

Central to the view of the civic capitalists is their belief that individuals ought to be morally responsible in all circumstances. Their ideal society is one based as far as possible on the free consent of all participants, rather than obedience to command. The idea of personal responsibility on which the ideal rests has three main elements. It is in part a pragmatic judgement that if people reap the rewards of their own success and bear the costs of their own mistakes, better results will follow for all. Second, it assumes that without standards against which we can constantly measure ourselves, human folly is more likely to prevail. And thirdly, it is based on the belief that a free society is superior to any alternative because it encourages people to demand much from one another. This view is in turn based on the optimistic belief that individuals are always capable of more, and on the moral imperative that we should all live our lives as an endeavour to leave the world a little better than we found it.

The underlying question is how people understand the human condition. Are we mere role performers, as in an enterprise association, or are we intelligent agents acting according to guiding principles? As Oakeshott put it, the individual in a nation of civil associates is:

> an intelligent agent understanding (or misunderstanding) his situation and responding to it in terms of wants and choices of actions and related to others in bargaining for satisfactions, in the co-operative pursuit of common wants, and in the recognition of moral and prudential procedures and practices.

The person is a 'free agent' as distinguished from a 'composition of biological or other urges'.[1]

As Hayek has shown, the idea of personal responsibility is intended to improve people, both the individuals directly involved and others who may learn from their successes or failures. If personal responsibility is weakened we may learn the wrong things. To hide failure is to mislead others and to damage their life chances. This is not a doctrine of meanness, nor of callous disregard. People who suffer through their own folly should be helped, but not in such a way as to conceal the results, which serves only to send the wrong signals to others. To conceal the costs of folly suppresses the process by which we learn from our mistakes.

Writers such as Acton did not think that 'society' was unimportant or that people were 'isolated individuals'. On the contrary, civic capitalists understood that some social systems are more consistent with good character than others. Communism, for instance, has tended to undermine honesty and commitment to others as people learned to employ deceit and subterfuge to survive in the face of terror.

The civic capitalists were first and foremost concerned to discover those common institutions, both private and public, which, on the one hand, encouraged individuals to become better citizens and which, on the other, reduced the harm that would result when human behaviour fell short of the ideal. Individuals are capable of great self sacrifice and many have laid down their own life for the good of others, but they are also capable of great wickedness. The civic capitalists were idealists whose vision was tempered by their awareness of human fallibility. As Professor Alfred Marshall wrote, 'progress mainly depends on the extent to which the strongest, and not merely the highest, forces of human nature can be utilised for the increase of social good'.[2]

Unlike some conservative thinkers who have celebrated established authority *per se*, civic capitalists did not forget that authority is a means and not an end. Nor was the purpose of government only to prevent crime. Its primary purpose was to foster liberty, by which they meant to create an environment in which people could fruitfully co-operate with one another. This is what the American founding fathers meant when they declared in the preamble to the American constitution that the purpose of government was to 'promote the general welfare and secure the blessings of liberty'.

The Family and Voluntary Associations

The civic capitalists were also aware that liberty rested on a good deal of voluntary restraint, which in turn depended on strong families in which children are raised to be good citizens of a liberal society, and on a vigorous civil society of voluntary associations of every kind in which people work with others to achieve common ends and to promote virtue in one another.

This is the prime importance of voluntary associations. They may provide services better or worse than any alternative, but their chief value lies in the opportunities they provide for the development of good qualities in the men and women whose strength of character fosters and maintains liberty against its enemies. Totalitarianism hates those strong characters whose high ideals lead them to resist tyranny. The ideal of liberty is about discovering just those institutions which serve as proving grounds for intellectual qualities such as seeking the truth and openness to contradiction, moral qualities such as honesty, service and self-sacrifice, and active qualities such as courage and determination, on which freedom ultimately depends.

The Legend of Liberty and the Reality

Opponents of capitalism frequently caricature it in order to discredit it. Two main caricatures have proved tenacious.

The first is that capitalism is no more than *laissez-faire* economics. But the approach of the civic capitalists examined here can not rightly be called *laissez faire*. They did not desire small government *per se*, but sought government of a particular *character*. Their view is not easy to summarise, but the essential question they asked about any government activity, existing or proposed, was: 'Are people being treated as means to the achievement of the government's ends, or is the government making means available to people to pursue their own ends'? No single-sentence, all-purpose principle can sum up civic capitalism and the emphasis on means in the previous sentence has its limitations but it has the merit of suggesting the direction our efforts ought to take in seeking to limit government. The ends of government can take various forms. Sometimes government is guided by a grand vision. It intends to create a better world and needs a dictatorship in the short run to force people to change. In other cases it has no overarching vision but becomes the tool of a special interest. The aim of government is to advance the interest of the group against others. The idea of limited government is an alternative to these other styles. In the seventeenth and eighteenth centuries it was in large part seen as a kind of truce between special interests and especially rival religions.

Later, in the twentieth century, it was presented as an alternative to communist and fascist dictatorships. But 'limited government' is not an end in itself. The objective of civic capitalists was to discern the style of government consistent with liberty.

The second caricature is that classical liberals or free marketeers advocate selfishness, indeed that their approach is rooted in selfishness. In *Past and Present*, published in 1843, Thomas Carlyle set the tone of much anti-capitalist rhetoric. His caricature of capitalism as based on the 'cash nexus' alone is still repeated. For instance, Professor Raymond Plant claims that under what he calls individualist conservatism: 'What matters is the result of a person's endeavours and whether others are prepared to pay for it. This is the *only* criterion of value applicable in a free society'.[3] Markets, he goes on to say, 'must be kept in their place', because they encourage 'egoism over altruism, and rational calculation of advantage over trust.'[4]

Frequently the capitalist tradition is presented as 'conservatism', or lately as Thatcherism. For instance, Ted Honderich, a professor of philosophy at the University of London, writes that:

> Conservatives remain fond of Adam Smith's pious discerning of a hidden hand in our affairs. This is the speculation ... that if each of us seeks selfishly our own personal profit, this may somehow and mysteriously serve a general end.[5]

The conclusion he reaches is that the conservative rationale for their politics is 'selfishness':

> Their selfishness alone is what explains their various and more important commitments in connection with property and a market, commitments to such things as reward. It explains their resistance to ... decent lives for those who lack them.[6]

This caricature of liberty bears no resemblance to the arguments of classical liberal writers such as Adam Smith, J.S. Mill, Tocqueville, Acton and Alfred Marshall, nor to its modern champions, Hayek and Novak. Classical liberals did not see people as consumers, with no more than a monetary motive. Their philosophy was one of respect for individuality in all its lawful manifestations.

Civic capitalists were not soft on selfishness. There are repeated examples of classical liberals seeking, in Marshall's terminology, to harness both the *strongest* and the *highest* motives of human conduct. Tocqueville contrasts 'self-interest rightly understood' with the older aristocratic ideal of selfless duty, a view which asserted that it was praiseworthy to serve others without hope of reward.[7] The idea of serving others without expectation of reward, Tocqueville reported from his visit to America in 1831 and 1832, was not popular in that country, but the same result was achieved by harnessing self-interest. It was typically argued that 'man serves himself in serving his fellow creatures and that his private interest is to do good'. In America 'hardly anybody talks of the beauty of virtue, but they maintain that virtue is useful and prove it every day', said Tocqueville. Men were not urged to sacrifice themselves for their fellows because it was noble, but because such sacrifices were useful to both parties.[8] Tocqueville cites Montaigne's dictum that, 'Were I not to follow the straight road for its straightness, I should follow it for having found by experience that in the end it is commonly the happiest and most useful track'.

So, according to Tocqueville, people were taught to be considerate towards others not because such conduct would bring its reward in heaven, but because they would enjoy success here on earth. American preachers taught 'self-interest rightly understood' by stressing the benefits here and now:

> To touch their congregations, they always show them how favourable religious opinions are to freedom and public tranquillity; and it is often difficult to ascertain from their discourses whether the principal object of religion is to procure eternal felicity in the other world or prosperity in this.[9]

This ethos demanded fewer acts of romantic self-sacrifice but suggested daily small acts of self-denial: it disciplined persons in habits of regularity, temperance, moderation, foresight, and self-command.

But according to Tocqueville, self-interest rightly understood by itself 'cannot suffice to make a man virtuous', and he was by no means satisfied. He thought self-interest rightly understood was much to be preferred to 'self-interest *wrongly* understood', that is plain selfishness; and superior to 'individualism', a term he used in the special sense of retreating into private pre-occupations. In some countries the inhabitants, he thought: 'set too high a value upon their time to spend it on the interests of the community; and they shut themselves up in narrow selfishness, marked out by four sunk fences and a quickset hedge'.[10]

Indeed, few civic capitalists were satisfied merely with appeals to self-interest rightly understood. They also urged the highest idealism. Adam Smith was very clear that a framework of law was vital to a free society, but knew that law alone could not create the good society. Justice, said Adam Smith was 'the main pillar that upholds the whole edifice',[11] but people should also seek to do right according to conscience:

> That the sense of duty should be the sole principle of our conduct, is nowhere the precept of Christianity; but that it should be the ruling and the governing one, as philosophy, and as, indeed, common sense, directs.[12]

And Smith left no room for doubt about his own hopes for humankind:

> to feel much for others, and little for ourselves, that to restrain our selfish, and to indulge our benevolent, affections, constitutes the perfection of human nature; and can alone produce among mankind that harmony of sentiments and passions in which consists their whole grace and propriety.[13]

Acton put conscience at the very core of his conception of liberty, contrasting the 'reign of authority' with the 'reign of conscience'. This is how he described the attitude of the seventeenth century religious rebels against the divine authority of kings:

> It appeared to them that governments and institutions are made to pass away, like the things of earth, whilst souls are immortal; that there is no more proportion between liberty and power than between eternity and time; that, therefore, the sphere of enforced command ought to be restricted within fixed limits, and that which had been done by authority, and outward discipline, and organised violence, should be attempted by division of power, and committed to the intellect and the conscience of free men.[14]

Thus, for Acton, to narrow the reach of authority was to widen the scope of conscience. This is almost the reverse image of the legend of capitalism often propagated today whereby the realm of government is proclaimed the realm of altruism and the realm of the private condemned as that of selfishness or egotism.

Nothing is Sacred: Modern Neglect of the Moral Foundations

A fundamental defect of the economic rationalism which came to dominance in the 1980s is its lack of respect for the sacred, but this narrowness is now coming under attack, not by conservative opponents of liberty who prefer authority to conscience, but by champions of freedom who want to see liberty firmly rooted in the consciences of free men and women.

For Michael Novak the chief danger to the West lies in neglecting the spiritual side of human nature. He believes there is a malaise at the heart of modern thought, not least because the focus on the material advantages of markets has led inadvertently to neglect of the 'inner life' of free citizens. This neglect has had heavy costs, measured by deteriorating standards of personal behaviour, such as rising crime—reflecting a lower respect for other people and their possessions—and growing illegitimacy—reflecting a lower willingness of men to be good fathers to the children they have sired. Like many before him his concern is with character:

> Character is the bundle of acquired moral and intellectual powers through which each person slowly fashions his or her unique capacity for insight and choice. Character is the self-appropriation of one's own liberty. A person of character is a person in charge of his or her own life, moved from within, a self-mastering agent.[15]

Character is moulded first and foremost within the family and we have yet to count the full cost of its diminishing importance, an issue to which I return in Chapter 11.

Summary

The founders of civic capitalism saw the state as the protector of the people from crime and oppression as well as the facilitator of human ingenuity. They saw individuals as each struggling to understand the world around them and to make the most of their own lives in mutual concert with others. No less important, they saw people as united, not in pursuit of a uniform goal, since all were free to pursue their own objectives, but by the particular sense of solidarity that results from a shared awareness of belonging to a civilisation that gives everyone their chance. Solidarity is a term generally associated with egalitarianism, or with the creation of cohesion through compulsory transfers of cash—as exemplified by the European Community's 'cohesion fund'—but the solidarity associated with liberty is the sense of unity that flows from being part of a culture that respects persons as fully entitled to make the most of the opportunities available to them and which expects each individual to uphold the values on which freedom rests.[16] To feel love for their country has been typical of free citizens, as demonstrated by the high morale of the allied soldiers of World War II.

Also central to the thinking of civic capitalists has been a commitment to personal responsibility, partly for prudential and partly for moral reasons. They thought it prudent for people to be free to pursue their own lawful ends as their judgement dictated and at their own risk, because better results in the interests of all were more likely. This view was taken partly because, when decision makers spend other people's money, they do not exercise the same care as when they personally bear the cost of failure or reap the reward of success. In addition, classical liberals believed that the personal bearing of risk gave individuals a powerful reason to improve their knowledge, skills and character. Morally, their view was based on the argument that freedom will not work unless we all accept an obligation to treat others with the respect due to fellow moral agents.

Part II

The Lived Reality of Liberty

3

The Evolution of Mutual Aid

Most histories of welfare provision tend to equate the improvement of welfare services with the growth of government involvement.[1] Over the years the welfare state filled the gaps supposedly left by the market. More careful examination of the evidence, however, shows that the reality was very different. People in need because of their inability to earn enough to support themselves, whether temporarily or permanently, were supported in a rich variety of ways. Family and neighbours played their part but because their help was informal and undocumented historians have tended to underestimate it. Charity was also important and it is often supposed that organised welfare before the welfare state was left to charities, but by far the most important organised method by which people met the needs of their fellows was mutual aid. In Britain the friendly societies were the most important providers of social welfare during the nineteenth and early twentieth centuries.

The friendly societies were self-governing mutual benefit associations founded by manual workers to provide against hard times. They strongly distinguished their guiding philosophy from the philanthropy which lay at the heart of charitable work. The mutual benefit association was not run by one set of people with the intention of helping another separate group, it was an association of individuals pledged to help each other when the occasion arose. Any assistance was not a matter of largesse but of entitlement, earned by the regular contributions paid into the common fund by every member and justified by the obligation to do the same for other members if hardship came their way. They began as local clubs, holding their common fund in a wooden chest or strong-box, but the nineteenth century saw the gradual evolution of national federations with hundreds of thousands of members and carefully managed investments.

During the nineteenth century and until early this century most families took pride in being self supporting but wages were such that, if the breadwinner fell ill or died, hardship was the invariable result. The philosophy forged by this harsh reality was mutual aid. By the early years of this century the friendly societies had a long record of functioning as social and benevolent clubs as well as offering benefits: such as sick pay when the breadwinner was unable to bring home a wage due to illness, accident or old age; medical care for both the member and his family; a death grant sufficient to provide a decent funeral; and financial and practical support for widows and orphans of deceased members. Medical services were usually provided by the lodge or branch doctor who was appointed by a vote of the members, but most large towns also had a medical institute, offering the services now provided by health centres. The societies also provided a network of support to enable members to travel in search of work. These services are described in Chapter 5.

The first Act of Parliament dealing specifically with friendly societies described them as societies

> of good fellowship for the purpose of raising from time to time, by subscriptions of the several members ... a stock or fund for the mutual relief and maintenance of all and every the members thereof, in old age, sickness, and infirmity, or for the relief of the widows and children of deceased members.

This description comes from the Act for the Encouragement and Relief of Friendly Societies passed in 1793.[2] Of course, friendly societies existed long before this Act was passed. Among the oldest was the Incorporation of Carters, founded in 1555 at Leith in Scotland, but it was not until the eighteenth century that the number of societies expanded rapidly.

Membership of the friendly societies grew steadily during the eighteenth century. By 1801 an authoritative study by Sir Frederic Eden estimated that there were about 7,200 societies with around 648,000 adult male members out of a total population of about nine million. This can be compared with a figure based on the Poor Law return for 1803 when it was estimated that there were 9,672 societies with 704,350 members in England and Wales alone.[3]

By the time the British Government came to introduce compulsory social insurance for 12 million persons under the 1911 National Insurance Act, at least 9 million were already covered by registered and unregistered voluntary insurance associations, chiefly the friendly societies. In 1910, the last full year before the 1911 Act, there were 6.6 million members of registered friendly societies, quite apart from those not registered (discussed in Chapter 6). The rate of growth of the friendly societies over the preceding thirty years had been accelerating.[4] In 1877, registered membership had been 2.75 million. Ten years later it was 3.6 million, increasing at an average of 85,000 a year. In 1897 membership had reached 4.8 million, having increased on average by 120,000 a year. And by 1910 the figure had reached 6.6 million, having increased at an annual average rate since 1897 of 140,000.

It was at the height of their expansion that the state intervened and transformed the friendly societies by introducing compulsory national insurance—but more on this in Chapter 9.

Origins

At first the societies were local gatherings of men who knew each other and who met regularly to socialise, usually at a public house. All members paid a regular contribution which gave them an agreed entitlement to benefit. Some divided any surplus annually, often just before Christmas; others accumulated funds beyond a year. Some of the societies had no written rules; others had elaborate rulebooks. Each society was completely autonomous and it was this self-governing character which was always one of the strongest attractions to members. They were organisations which could be speedily adapted in any way to meet members' needs as and when they arose. When the government introduced a scheme for registration, very many societies preferred not to register, because to do so meant putting a legal limitation on their ability to adapt. As P.H. Gosden, the leading historian of the friendly societies, comments: 'If a majority of the members wanted to spend part of their contributions on an annual feast they were not prepared to put themselves in the position where agents of the government might try to prevent them from doing so'.[5]

The Rise of the Federations

Many early clubs were organised as dividing societies, that is each member paid an equal amount into the common fund and if there was a surplus after the payment of benefits at the end of the year, it was divided up equally among members. Such societies retained their popularity well into the twentieth century, but their disadvantages soon became apparent. First, the lack of an accumulated fund meant that they sometimes ran out of cash, and second, because of the annual renewal of membership very sick people were sometimes excluded at the year's end. These flaws led to the emergence of federations with accumulated reserves and a right to continued membership so long as contributions were paid.

Federations began to develop from early in the nineteenth century and became known as affiliated orders. By the time of the Royal Commission on the Friendly Societies of 1874 there were 34 of them with over 1,000 members each, with the Manchester Unity of Odd-fellows and the Ancient Order of Foresters alone accounting for nearly a million members between them.

Sometimes the growth of federations was the result of a central organisation setting up new branches and sometimes of local sick clubs banding together or joining an existing federation. The largest society, the Manchester Unity of Oddfellows was founded by Robert Naylor who, along with other friends, had been holding meetings for convivial purposes at the Ropemakers' Arms in Salford. In 1810 a regular branch called the Abercrombie lodge was established, and Robert Naylor became the Manchester Unity's founding member. Membership expanded fast and new lodges were opened. Between 1810 and 1814 Abercrombie lodge also encouraged existing lodges to accept their leadership. The first record of a union of lodges, formed 'for the purpose of affording each other mutual support, protection and advice', is for the year 1814. From that time the Independent Order of Oddfellows, Manchester Unity grew rapidly. In 1838 it had 90,000 members; by 1848, 249,000; and by 1876, just over half a million.

The emergence of federations had considerable implications for the internal government of the societies. The prevailing ethic in the earliest clubs was that everyone should have an equal say in common decisions. And since it was possible for all the members to meet in one place the normal practice was for decisions to be taken in a general assembly of all members. These early meetings were not only to reach decisions, but also for enjoyment, as the rules of the early clubs reflect. Invariably, they provide for the maintenance of order as well as the distribution of beer to members.

The early institutions of manual workers tried out several different methods of self-government. First, there was the referendum:

33

members who could not all meet in one place could still all vote. Second, there was the solution of having a governing branch, with power rotating from branch to branch. Third, there was the delegate meeting, each delegate being closely bound by the instructions of his constituents. Fourth was the representative assembly, comprising elected members free to take the decisions they believed best, in the light of the facts of which they were aware and their constituents' wishes or interests as they saw them.

Gradually, a three-tier federal structure emerged—branch, district and unity—which combined significant local autonomy with representation at district and unity (national) levels. In the affiliated orders the branches—known as lodges among the Oddfellows and courts among the Foresters—retained wide powers, though final decision-making authority rested with an annual or biennial assembly. This assembly was known by different titles in different orders, though most retained the tradition of a movable meeting to guard against the emergence of a geographical centre of power. In the Manchester Unity of Oddfellows the governing body was originally known as the Annual Movable Committee; in the Ancient Order of Foresters the High Court; in the Independent Order of Rechabites, Salford Unity the High Movable Conference; and in the Grand United Order of Oddfellows as the Biennial Movable Delegation. Each assembly was empowered to make, annul, or amend the rules of the order. And each concluded with the election of the president, and the executive committee, which usually comprised the chief officers and between six and a dozen other members.

The most important duty of the executive committee in any order was to supervise the management of the districts and lodges. It was obliged to examine the books and accounts, to protect minority interests in the lodges, and to ensure that the society's rules were observed. It also acted as a final court of appeal for disputes which could not be settled in lodges or at district level. The chairman of the executive committee, who was also the president of the order, was usually appointed for one year. He was given various titles: Grand Master, High Court Ranger, Chief Shepherd, Most Worthy Patriarch and High Chief Ruler.

The most important official was the Grand Secretary, sometimes with that title, at other times variously called the Corresponding Secretary, Permanent Secretary, or High Court Scribe. The societies prided themselves on the absence of barriers to the advancement of any member to senior office:

> the rights of every individual member are scrupulously respected and
> guarded; each individual has equal rights and privileges; merit alone is
> the medium through which posts of honour may be arrived at, and no
> artificial barriers are permitted to prevent virtue and talent from occupy-
> ing their fitting station.[6]

And just as labour parties in Western democracies demanded that
parliamentarians should be paid to permit wage earners to compete
on equal terms, so the friendly societies ensured that want of cash did
not deter their members from holding the highest offices.

It was only later in the nineteenth century that an intermediate
level of organisation was introduced between local branches and the
national level. It was found advisable to spread the liability for death
benefit more widely than amongst members of each branch, where
even a few deaths in rapid succession could exhaust a small fund.
Many societies evolved a district structure to spread the risk. Each
district took its authority direct from the central body, but was
governed by a committee of representatives from the individual
branches. Apart from controlling the funeral funds, the districts also
served as intermediate courts of appeal, and supervised the management of the various lodges, examining accounts and intervening
where necessary. Lodges were required to send in yearly balance
sheets and reports, to the district as well as to the central body.[7]
However, some branches disliked the additional control that the
district system entailed, and refused to affiliate.

By the mid-nineteenth century this process of evolution from the
local club with its participatory democracy to the three-tier structure
with a representative assembly and a full-time chief executive officer
was well under way. But the original ideal of pure democracy
retained much force and was often the yardstick against which
proposed changes in the decision-making structure were judged.
During the heyday of the autonomous local sick club it was generally
held that everyone was equally well-equipped to hold office, a
common belief in other working-class organisations, especially when
new. For example, in a leading article in the *Clarion* published soon
after the establishment of the Independent Labour Party in 1893, the
editor (in the view of Sidney Webb the most influential member of
that party) declared:

> It is tolerably certain that in so far as the ordinary duties of officials and

delegates, such as committee men or members of Parliament, are concerned, an average citizen, if he is thoroughly honest, will be found quite clever enough to do all that is needful... Let all officials be retired after one year's services, and fresh ones elected in their place.[8]

The friendly societies retained much of this spirit, and over many years structures evolved which balanced the need for competent performance of organisational duties and the desire for the maximum participation of members. But this strong commitment to vigorous local democracy did not mean that the desire of members to participate could be taken for granted. The Grand United Order of Oddfellows found it necessary to emphasise the importance of participation to members undergoing initiation:

> Whoever enters this Order for the mean and selfish object of paying his contributions and receiving its pecuniary benefits, without, so far as in him lies, aiding in the arduous labours of conducting the business of his Lodge, is to be regarded as an unworthy intruder; but we trust that you will run a nobler and a truer course; proving by your conduct that you are worthy of the Order.[9]

Not that such appeals were always heeded. By the end of the century complaints in the friendly society magazines indicate many branches were finding it difficult to secure good attendances at meetings. From the beginning lodges fined members for non-attendance of lodge meetings. The 1907 rules of the *Robert Gordon* branch of the Foresters, based in North Shields, laid down that members residing within two miles of the court meeting place in the *Clock Vaults* in Wellington Street, would have to pay a fine of 3d for absence at quarterly summoned meetings, unless they gave a satisfactory written apology.[10] Members were also required to pay their contributions on the meeting night. In the Foresters, for example, the usual rule was that contributions must be paid to the secretary on court nights and at no other time. But some members just looked in to pay and then left. Others waited till the end of the quarter, by which time contributions *had* to be paid, and then called in briefly to pay.

The Societies and Participatory Democracy

The friendly societies are of special interest because they sought to combine a high level of control by individual members with efficient administration. The welfare state is commonly criticised for excessive centralisation but this has not been a problem faced only by governments. Once the affiliated orders had ceased to be purely local clubs, the balance of power between the centre and the branches was a constant concern.

The affiliated societies produced a number of unique solutions to this age-old problem, solutions which minimised the costs and maximised the advantages for efficiency which a high level of participation can bring. The approach taken by the Foresters was that all lawful authority originated 'with and from the Members at large'. Power in the members, says the Foresters' first lecture, 'is like the light of the Sun—native, original, inherent, and unlimited by anything human. Power in our Officers is only borrowed, delegated, and limited by the intention of the Members, whose it is, and to whom all officials are responsible.' In the branch, all Foresters met on equal terms:

> In the Court, and before the law, no one is greater than another. All meet there on terms of perfect equality... No office is too high for the poorest to aspire to; no duty too humble for the richest to stoop to. Intelligence to govern, ability to exercise authority with becoming humility, yet with the requisite firmness, and personal demeanour to ensure respect, are all the qualifications for office required; and these are in the power of every Member to acquire.[11]

The early clubs gave the branch chairman the power to impose fines for misconduct and the affiliated orders followed their example. The Foresters' Court *Old Abbey*, based in Guisborough, empowered its chief ranger to fine members 3d for interrupting another or 6d for swearing or using abusive or insulting language.[12]

At the same time, the federations as well as the early clubs were keenly aware of the need to prevent presiding officers from abusing their power. Most societies impressed their expectations on a new chairman at his installation ceremony. The chief ranger in the Foresters took the following oath on assuming office:

> I, [name], having been elected Chief Ranger hereby solemnly promise and declare before you and the Brethren present, that I will do all within my power to promote the general welfare, peace and harmony of the Court and that I will endeavour to act with impartiality in all matters connected with the office to which I have been appointed.[13]

In the Grand United Order of Oddfellows an incoming chairman (noble grand) was reminded of his responsibilities by the installing officer:

'Worthy and Respected Brother, in taking upon you the duties of Noble Grand, do you feel that you are taking upon yourself a serious responsibility?'

'I do.'

'Are you willing and determined to discharge your duties with faithfulness, and without prejudice or partiality to any one?'

'I am.'

'Your qualifications should be of the highest order. In the first place, you should have a thorough knowledge of the Laws by which, as Oddfellows, we are governed. It would be well, therefore, if you would rigidly examine yourself in this respect, so that, if deficient, you may vigilantly apply yourself to study ...'

'One who holds your office should have an affable and temperate disposition; he should be able to look with composure upon a moral tempest, unruffled by its rage, contemplating only how he may repress its violence, and produce a calm. Whilst strict, he should be gentle; whilst firm, untainted by severity; and in wielding the instruments of justice, he should always aim at the spot whence spring reflection and moral consciousness.'[14]

The societies did not wholly rely upon moral appeals. Rules also laid down what a chairman could and could not do. The *General Laws* of the Foresters, for example, stipulate that if the presiding officer vacated his chair 'without permission of the assembled brethren, or without first providing some competent person to succeed him', or refused to put to the vote 'any proposition that has been legally made', he could, if the offence was not 'so flagrant as to cause a motion for his deposition', be fined five shillings for the first offence, ten shillings for the second, and up to 21s for subsequent offences.[15]

A stronger method of preventing abuse was to provide for an officer to be instantly deposed. The Foresters provided:

> That in order to make every officer responsible to his constituents for the becoming and faithful discharge of his trust, and more readily to check insolent demeanour, or to prevent any abuse of power ... the assembled High Court or any District or subordinate Court, shall have the power of ... immediately deposing him or them.[16]

In a number of societies the lodge opening ceremony also served to inhibit the tendency for officeholders to become too powerful. In Manchester Unity, at the beginning of every meeting, each office holder was required solemnly to state the duties he owed to lodge members. The elective secretary was required to recite his duties as follows: 'To enter every particular transaction, or minute, without prejudice, and explain the same when required by you [the chairman] or a majority of the Lodge.' The financial secretary, in his turn, had to say: 'To keep a fair and impartial account between every member and the Lodge; to explain and balance such whenever required by you or a majority of the Lodge, and as far as in my power lies to keep the accounts clear and intelligible.'[17]

In the early clubs the rotation of office was employed to ensure a sharing of the burdens and advantages of office, but gradually rotation gave way to regular elections. In the Manchester Unity, for example, with the exception of the financial secretary who held office at the pleasure of the lodge, it was customary for leading offices to change hands at each six-monthly or annual election.

Training Grounds for Democracy

Each friendly society had its peculiarities. But the affiliated orders share a tradition and are, for most purposes, comparable. In the Manchester Unity the new member was eligible for any of the assistant offices: warden, guardian, conductor and assistant secretary. The guardian's task was to guard the door and ensure that the correct password was given. The conductor helped new members through the initiation ceremony. The warden examined each person in attendance to establish their right to be present, and had custody of lodge regalia. Each lodge also had two secretaries, the elective secretary and the financial secretary. The main task of the elective secretary was to take the minutes of the meetings. Each of these positions, except that of financial secretary, was expected to change hands at every election.

The financial secretary was elected at a summoned meeting —held once per quarter and to which every member had to receive a written invitation at least seven days in advance—and thereafter held office at the pleasure of the lodge. It was usual for lodges to try to find a competent person and keep him in this position for it was on his shoulders that the main duties fell. Sometimes branches found it difficult to come by a capable secretary. This was one of the costs of self-organisation. Many branches were made up of members skilled in manual occupations but with no experience of administrative work. And embezzlement was not unknown.

In addition to the two secretaries, each lodge also had three major offices: the noble grand or chairman, the vice grand or vice-chairman and the immediate past noble grand. These offices changed hands regularly. All members were expected to seek to occupy these positions—to 'go through the chairs' as it was called—and were required to prove themselves by holding the minor offices and by taking the degrees of the order (Chapter 4). To be eligible for election as the vice grand a member must have held two assistant offices, served as elective secretary, and taken two minor degrees. To be eligible for the position of noble grand a member must have taken all four minor degrees, have served as vice grand, and be able to deliver the lectures 'in a proper manner'.

But what was expected was not mere turn-taking. The holding of office was also a process by which the member could learn new skills. And for many manual workers the lodge offered opportunities for self-improvement lacking at the workplace. But the policy of changing the chairman every six months also carried with it the risk that the newcomer might be incompetent. To overcome this danger and to ensure that ready advice was available to the novice, each noble grand would appoint two supporters, a right and left supporter. They would sit on either side of him at meetings and whisper advice as the meeting proceeded. Traditionally, the noble grand chose an experienced right supporter, a member who had previously held the office and who was well informed about the rules and procedures. The left supporter was a friend whose task was to give unflinching moral support. In this fashion a high level of sharing of office was combined with efficient performance. And manual workers, whose role in the workplace was perhaps mundane and narrow were able to develop their talents and share in the satisfaction of knowing that they were doing their bit to maintain the ideal of mutual service which inspired the friendly society movement.

On completing a term as noble grand the member automatically served a term as the immediate past noble grand. Neither the noble grand nor the immediate past noble grand were permitted to stand for election as noble grand until twelve months had elapsed. The vice grand was also ineligible to stand again for the position of vice grand. This ensured a high level of turnover and made it more difficult for the lodge to be dominated by a self-appointed clique. There was also a provision preventing district officers from holding elective lodge offices which helped to ensure the independence of lodges from the district organisation.

A member who had held lodge offices could seek to hold still higher positions. An individual who had served in the four minor offices, taken the minor degrees, served as vice grand, noble grand and immediate past noble grand, became eligible to sit for the past grand's degree, or purple degree. If successful he became a member of the past grand's lodge and was eligible to hold office at the district and unity levels. The district officers were, the district secretary, district grand master, district deputy grand master and immediate past district grand master.

Above the district was, the grand master, the deputy grand master and the immediate past grand master. These positions were subject to annual elections. The board of directors comprised these three officers and nine other individuals elected by the annual conference. They retired annually but could stand for re-election. Each was required to hold the purple degree. The grand secretary was a full-time appointee, elected initially by the annual conference and holding office at its pleasure.

Respect for Rules and for Each Other

The leading societies invariably had an elaborate rulebook, which was almost an object of reverence to the manual workers who made up the membership. Before the rules every member was equal. Moreover, the rules were not externally imposed, they had been fashioned over the years by the members themselves: adopted, adapted, annulled and revised regularly as circumstances changed. If the rules imposed constraints, as they must, they were constraints freely accepted by every member.

Friendly society members were proud of their rules. They were proud, not of the rules *per se*, but of the principles they embodied. The rules laid down what every member must contribute and what his rights were, and stipulated the duties of office holders. They limited the powers of office holders and ensured a sharing of the pleasures and burdens of office. And the rules maintained the autonomy of the branches from the district and unity levels within each federation. The societies were in a real sense ruled by laws rather than ruled by men, and to that extent they were admirable training grounds for participation in the democratic process of the nation.

The Friendly Societies at the Turn of the Century

During the latter part of the nineteenth century new types of society began to develop as conditions changed. When classifying the types of society it is customary to distinguish between societies which provided sickness benefit (general societies) and those which did not (specialised societies). The payment of sickness benefit was for most societies their biggest single task.

In 1910, before the 1911 National Insurance Act had made its impact, there were 26,877 societies of all types with 6,623,000 registered members.[18] The general societies are sub-divided into: orders and branches; unitary accumulating societies; dividing societies; and deposit or Holloway societies.

Table 1

Registered Membership of General Friendly Societies in 1910

	No. of branches or societies	Members
Orders and Branches	20,580	2,782,953
Unitary Accumulating	3,117	1,277,185
Dividing Societies	1,335	292,909
Deposit and Holloway	81	381,491
Total		**4,734,538**

Source: Beveridge, *Voluntary Action*, Table 21.

Total membership of special friendly societies in 1910 was 1,888,178, of which 855,962 were in death and burial societies, 403,190 in societies providing for shipwreck and miscellaneous losses and 329,450 in societies providing medical care.[19] A fuller discussion of registered and unregistered membership follows in Chapter 6. The remainder of this chapter concentrates on the various types of society which evolved.

Dividing Societies

According to Beveridge, three aspirations contributed to the formation of friendly societies: the first was the desire for security in sickness, the second a desire to avoid a pauper funeral, and the third to save a lump sum for emergencies, old age or spending on a substantial item.[20] The affiliated orders were primarily concerned with sick pay, medical care and funeral benefit, though as the nineteenth century progressed they directed their attention more towards deferred annuities for old age and endowment assurance.

The dividing societies, however, laid greater stress on saving and shared any annual surplus among members. The weakness of the dividing principle was that as the members aged the benefits got larger and the annual surplus smaller. But this lack of actuarial calculation was also its advantage. By paying a higher contribution than was strictly necessary, members knew that the benefits would usually be covered and that any surplus would be returned to them. It also provided a good check on malingering, since each member had an interest in a surplus remaining at the year's end. Beveridge quotes the evidence given to the Royal Commission of 1874 by the Reverend Portman of Steeple Fitzpaine in Somerset. He acknowledged that it might initially seem improvident to divide the surplus each year, but drew attention to the advantages. A 'lump' of money of twenty-five or thirty shillings now and then was a great boon to the agricultural labourers. And he had found it was not wastefully spent, but rather used to purchase an item such as a pig, or shoes or clothing. According to Beveridge, 'The whole of rural England is or was a collection of Steeple Fitzpaines'.[21]

Deposit Societies

The same desire for a balance between saving, on the one hand, and security in sickness and provision against death, on the other, led to the formation of deposit and Holloway societies. The earliest deposit society was founded in 1831, but the idea did not catch on until later. In 1868 a society was formed at Albury in Surrey which in 1872 became the National Deposit Friendly Society, by far the largest of its type. Each member made a contribution which, after a deduction for management, went partly to a common fund for sick pay and partly to a personal account which accumulated at interest. Members could choose the size of their contribution so long as it was no less than 2s per month and no more than 20s. This contribution then determined the benefit: the daily rate of sick benefit was the same as the monthly rate of contribution. In addition, each member was urged on joining to make an initial deposit to their personal account of between 3d and

£30. This deposit did not affect the rate of benefit, though it had an effect on its duration.

Sick pay was drawn partly from the common fund and partly from the member's personal account in a proportion which varied with age at joining. It was payable until the member's personal account was exhausted. This meant that a person who did not experience much illness would accumulate a large surplus by retirement age. It also meant that someone who was ill for long periods could exhaust his personal account, but in such cases the member received 'grace pay' for the same period that sick pay had already been drawn. As a result of these incentives, the National Deposit Friendly Society had low sickness experience.

Benefits were paid as follows. Sick pay for males who joined between the ages of 16 and 30 was paid 25 per cent from their personal account and 75 per cent from the common fund. Grace pay was 75 per cent of benefit. Benefit for males who had joined when they were 40-50 was paid half from the common fund and half from the personal account and grace pay was half sick pay. Membership of the National Deposit Friendly Society in 1872 was about 1,000; in 1899, 46,000 and by 1910, 210,000.[22] After the introduction of national insurance the society grew rapidly and by 1939 it had 1,462,183 members.

Holloway Societies

Holloway societies were based on principles invented by George Holloway who, in 1874, founded the Working Men's Conservative Friendly Society in Stroud. It also combined saving and sick pay but on different lines from the National Deposit Friendly Society. The contribution was substantially more than was necessary for sick pay and the whole contribution went into a common fund. Each year the surplus was divided equally and credited to personal accounts which earned interest. The contribution was the same for all aged up to 30 but increased each year thereafter. Holloway societies also differed in that an individual could increase his share of the distributed surplus by holding more than one share in the society (up to ten shares). The essential idea was to pay more than was necessary for sick pay in order to build up a surplus for old age. However, unlike the National Deposit Friendly Society, it was not possible to run out of sick pay. The two largest Holloway societies were the Ideal Benefit Society of

Birmingham (founded in 1893) and the Tunbridge Wells Equitable (founded in 1881).

Unitary Accumulating Societies

The accumulating societies without branches were thus named to distinguish them from dividing societies which did not accumulate funds for more than a twelve-month period. Most of the unitary accumulating societies were local in character, but one or two stood out from the crowd. Hearts of Oak was the largest of the unitary friendly societies. It started in 1842 with 12 members. By 1856 its membership was 5,000 and by 1872 it had grown to 32,000. It was governed by an assembly of delegates representing 231 areas into which the country was divided. Before 1911 an effort was made to keep alive the local spirit, but after national insurance such efforts were abandoned. It paid sick pay, death benefit and also offered endowment insurance. It prospered under national insurance, and at the beginning of World War II it had 444,000 members.[23]

Conclusion

Friendly societies, therefore, came in all shapes and sizes and it was this flexibility that formed an important part of their attraction. As Beveridge argued in *Voluntary Action*, it was remarkable how so many of the great institutions that proved popular began as a meeting of a dozen or so people in the evening after work, often in the back room of a public house. Some failed and some succeeded. In doing so, argued Beveridge, they changed the world:

> In a totalitarian State or in a field already made into a State monopoly, those dissatisfied with the institutions that they find can seek a remedy only by seeking to change the Government of the country. In a free society and a free field they have a different remedy; discontented individuals with new ideas can make a new institution to meet their needs. The field is open to experiment and success or failure; secession is the midwife of invention.[24]

4

Character-Building Associations

'Guardian, Tyle the Door!'—with these words the noble grand in the Manchester Unity of Oddfellows declares the lodge meeting open. He then enjoins the warden to examine everyone present cautioning: 'and if there be any of whom you have the least suspicion as not being entitled to be present, inform me thereof; be particular in your examination'.

Amidst silence, the warden proceeds. He knows most of those present, but new members are asked to give the password. We can share in the tension of the newcomer who, with all eyes on him, struggles to recall the password. He replies correctly. Other strangers are also challenged. If they all answer correctly the warden reports to the lodge chairman, 'All correct, most Noble Grand', and the meeting proceeds.[1]

In this fashion the atmosphere of the lodge is at once established. Here was not an ordinary meeting, but a gathering united by common ideals. This commitment to the building of shared idealism, to moulding good character and encouraging participation in the common work, was a feature of the affiliated orders, the biggest single group of friendly societies. But it was not part of the make-up of the centralised societies. They were more than mere business corporations, but they did not attach the same weight to conviviality and character building as the affiliated orders.

Just as affiliated friendly societies were not merely benefit societies so too it is a misunderstanding to see them as primarily neighbourhood associations. Their members were united not by their physical proximity but by their attachment to shared ideals. Central to the purpose of the societies was the promotion of good character, a consideration of great importance for classical-liberal thought, some of whose advocates tend to take good conduct and a desire for a better life for granted, and consequently to assume that every person will readily become an ambitious, self-reliant, participating citizen. In the 1860s and 1870s, when the poor law was becoming more lenient, the wholesome influence of the friendly societies and other institutions like the Methodist and non-conformist churches proved sufficient to maintain a strong commitment to liberty and self-reliance. In the years after World War Two, when such institutions had lost their influence, welfare leniency produced a different result, measured in family breakdown and growing personal dependency.

The friendly societies knew only too well that they had to cultivate the philosophy of self-help and mutual support which guided them, and great effort was put into keeping the tradition strong. It was achieved by encouraging members to enmesh themselves in the activities of the society and to share its ideals. In the leading societies, ideals were gradually revealed to members in the ritual. The very first experience of the new member was an initiation ceremony, when the values of the society were dramatically presented. These ceremonies have changed considerably over the years. It was only in 1843 that the Ancient Order of Foresters abandoned initiation by combat. Prior to that the candidate had been led in to the court room to be addressed by a chief ranger holding two cudgels. The chief ranger solemnly addressed the candidate:

'Stranger, we never admit of any becoming members of our ancient and honourable institution but those who are possessed of a bold, valiant, and enterprising spirit; and, therefore, before you can be admitted we must have some proof of your courage and ability. You may depend upon being used with the strictest honour.'

Presenting him with the cudgels, he added, 'Here are two such weapons as we generally make use of. Take them, make choice of one, and give the other to any of my worthy brothers in the room as your antagonist, and he will show you the use of them.'

The candidate did as he was instructed and as soon as one of the members had accepted the second cudgel, the chief ranger directed the court: 'Worthy Sub-Chief Ranger, Senior and Junior Woodwards, you will attend the combat, see the courage of the candidate fairly tried, according to ancient custom, and report the same to me.'

The candidate and his chosen opponent then set-to with the cudgels. If the candidate acquitted himself sufficiently well, it was the duty of the sub-chief ranger of the court to report the outcome.

'Worthy Chief Ranger, the courage of the candidate has been fairly tried, according to ancient custom, and he is found worthy.'[2]

In the later ceremonies, candidates were offered an account of the *raison d'être* of the society, and of the manner in which they would be expected to conduct themselves. These words were spoken to new members of the Ancient Order of Foresters:

> We are united together not only for the wise purpose of making provision against those misfortunes which befall all men, and of assisting those who require our aid, but for the moderate enjoyment of friendly intercourse, and the temperate interchange of social feeling... We encourage no excess in our meetings, and enforcing no creed in religion or code in politics, we permit neither wrangling nor dissension to mar our harmony or interrupt our proceedings.

And the Foresters did not confine their advice to the conduct of society business:

> In your domestic relationships we look to find you, if a husband, affectionate and trustful; if a father, regardful of the moral and material well-being of your children and dependants; as a son, dutiful and exemplary, and as a friend, steadfast and true.[3]

In the Grand United Order of Oddfellows the new member was encouraged to make the moment of joining not only a time of self-criticism, but also an occasion for the very remoulding of his character:

> It is desired that you should make the event of your Initiation a time for strict self-examination; and if you should find anything in your past life to amend, I solemnly charge you to set about that duty without delay,—let no immoral practice, idle action, or low and vulgar pursuit, be retained by you.[4]

When performed well, the initiation ceremony was often a source of inspiration to new members and was only his first taste of the ritual which would form a regular part of lodge life. The Manchester Unity and the Grand United Order of Oddfellows had a series of degrees which were progressively awarded to members as they came to play a fuller part in the running of the lodge. The degrees took the form of ceremonies lasting, perhaps, fifteen minutes. On each occasion the member received a lecture from the chairman, and was given a secret grip, sign and password. In the Grand United Order of Oddfellows there were three of these 'minor degrees', in the Manchester Unity, four. Other societies explained their ideals to members in a series of lectures, a series of seven, for instance, in the Ancient Order of Foresters.

At the heart of the friendly societies' creed was a commitment to fraternity. And there is ample evidence of struggle to make fraternalism a reality. Fraternity was an ideal to which members appealed as they debated lodge policy or went about their duties as office-holders. Amidst debates in the lodge room, and in exchanges of view in society magazines, appeals to brotherhood played a part. And not without success. Of course, the secret grips, signs and passwords served to promote this brotherly bond in addition to their practical value as proof of identity for members travelling in search of work (below p. 60).

Fraternity is not the only value to which mutual aid societies subscribed. We also find a strong adherence to liberty in their attitude towards friendly society rules: 'Our laws are just and liberal', read the introduction to the Foresters' *General Laws* of 1857. They are 'fashioned after the purest models of government, and the 'greatest amount of individual liberty, consistent with the general welfare of the whole, is secured to every member'.[5]

Membership of a friendly society gave the industrial worker a status his working life failed to offer. He might have to sell his labour to earn a living, but in the lodge room the member was much more than a mere wage labourer. He was a member of a fraternity committed to high ideals. In the lodge room there were no bosses.

The importance of the lodges in giving status and self respect to members should not be under estimated. Industrial methods of production brought with them greater prosperity for manual workers, but the specialisation which created economic growth also produced a narrowing of human experience. The fraternalism of the lodge and the opportunity to throw oneself into regular work on behalf of fellow members was a great bonus for those working men who found the discipline of factory and foreman onerous.

Mutual Aid is not Charity

All of the leading societies very carefully distinguished their willingness to help one another from charity. For example, the Foresters' third lecture begins with a story:

> At the battle of Zutphen, Sir Philip Sidney, weak and mortally wounded, was borne by his attendants to a bank, beneath the shade of an Oak. His thirst was intense, and he called for water, which was brought to him in a helmet. As he was about to apply it to his lips, a poor soldier was borne

past him, likewise wounded. He gazed with longing eyes at the water—for the thirst of death was upon him also. Sir Philip, without himself tasting, ordered his attendants to let the poor soldier drink; 'for,' said he, 'he has more need of it than I'.

The lecture continues:

That was BENEVOLENCE, for it was a kind act, performed to one in necessity, without any accompanying feeling of selfishness. Had Sir Philip shared that which was not necessary for himself, the act would have been one of kindness. Had he given out of his abundance what he could well have spared, it would have been an act of charity—but not an act of BENEVOLENCE... We are specially called upon, as members of a common Fraternity, to practise BENEVOLENCE in its noblest and highest forms.

And as always, these sentiments—benevolence, kindness, charity— were carefully distinguished from entitlement:

For certain benefits in sickness ... all the Brethren in common subscribe to one fund. That fund is our Bank; and to draw therefrom is the independent and manly right of every Member, whenever the contingency for which the funds are subscribed may arise, as freely as if the fund was in the hand of their own banker, and they had but to issue a cheque for the amount. These are not BENEVOLENCES—they are rights.[6]

These words enable us to understand why the appeal to 'rights' was popular in the early years of the welfare state. But in the voluntary associations which pre-dated the welfare state the link between personal payment and entitlement was clear. Once the state intervened 'rights' increasingly became entitlements to benefits at the expense of *other* people, and no longer the just reward of shared responsibility.

The Undeserving Should Not be Neglected

Closely associated with the view that the benefits of the order were the member's right—the just reward of foresight and prudence—was the obvious corollary that it was not everyone who had thus paid their way. What was the attitude of the societies to the undeserving few? The Manchester Unity set out its view in its first degree. It uses the term 'charity', however, in a different sense from the Foresters. In the passage which follows the term 'charity' is closer to the idea of 'benevolence' found in the Foresters' third lecture just quoted:

... in extending our charity we must endeavour to distinguish the really deserving, for those who willingly and professionally seek the charity of others forfeit all self-respect, and, in being content so to live, sacrifice personal dignity. In these cases, it will be our duty to see that the love of independence be awakened, as it is the basis of all virtue and honour.

Lest this should be misinterpreted, the lecture emphasises that:

those who unworthily seek assistance are not to be neglected if really in distress; the voice of misery, proceed from whence it may, should never be disregarded. However, after relieving the actual wants of these unhappy persons, we should endeavour to raise them from the degradation into which they have fallen, and make them richer in their own esteem. As it is better that ten guilty persons escape than that one innocent should suffer, so it is better that ten undeserving persons be assisted than that one worthy be neglected.[7]

Voluntary Combinations

That the societies placed a high value on individual autonomy is not in doubt. But this did not mean that everyone was to be left to his own devices, or that the friendly societies saw no value in collective action:

Forestry recognises and practically enforces the great truth, that man is not formed for himself alone; that he has been designed for far nobler purposes than the practice of selfishness, or for the satisfaction of his own single pleasure—that for so mean and narrow a purpose his endowments are too excellent, his capacities too large. Forestry, therefore, acting on the reality that man is a social being, dependent on his brethren for comfort, enjoyment, aid, and succour, endeavours so to develop and direct the best sympathies of our nature that human distress may be alleviated, anguish abated, suffering relieved, and affliction blunted.[8]

However, in all their pronouncements on the value of combination, it was assumed throughout that any such combination would be voluntary. The friendly societies that flourished during the nineteenth century were strictly voluntary associations.

There had been occasional attempts to impose friendly societies on particular groups of workers in Britain, usually by members of the governing classes who were motivated, at least in part, by anxiety over the rising poor rate. An Act of 1757 compelled coalheavers working on the River Thames to contribute to a friendly society to be administered by an alderman of the City of London. Employers were ordered by the Act to retain two shillings in the pound from the men's wages. These contributions covered the cost of administration, and benefits paid at the rate of seven shillings per week during sickness and sixpence per day in old age. Provision was also made for burial expenses and for a payment to the widows and orphans of deceased coalheavers. The Act was repealed in 1770, 'having been found ineffectual to answer the purposes intended'. A similar measure was enacted in 1792 to compel shippers and keelmen employed in the coal trade on the River Wear to join a friendly society. A compulsory deduction was made from the men's wages at the rate of one half-penny for each cauldron of coal carried in their keelboats. Benefits were paid for sickness and old age, and payments made to widows and orphans.[9]

The 'benefit members' of such societies played no part in management, whereas the friendly society proper was a self-governing institution for *mutual*, and not one-sided or charitable aid. Societies managed by the honourary members to the exclusion of the benefit members also attracted relatively little support.[10] Friendly society members did not want to be 'ordered about' by the governing classes; nor did they wish to be the beneficiaries of their charity. And they were justly proud that voluntary associations of manual workers had improved the lot of their fellows without assistance from the 'upper crust'.

Collectivism Undermines Character

During the late nineteenth and early twentieth centuries pressure to extend the power of the state grew, and friendly society leaders were foremost in warning of the dangers. Addressing the annual conference in 1909, the grand master of the Manchester Unity raised doubts about the proposal of Lloyd George to introduce German-style national insurance:

> I venture to assert that the vast majority of my fellow members and thousands upon thousands of members of other friendly societies are totally opposed to any government undertaking the provision of any form of invalidity or sickness insurance for the working classes of this country.

By that time the Manchester Unity had over 750,000 members. The grand master conceded that even in the friendly societies' own ranks, there were a small number who imagined that evils could be put right by 'smothering voluntary individual effort and relying entirely on the state'. But, such a view, he thought, disregarded the effects on character. The state could compel a man to contribute to state insurance, but this would not make him careful or thrifty, or a good citizen.[11] No less important, a state scheme would narrow the opportunities for people to acquire and employ the skills of self-organisation.

Such experience, said the Ancient Order of Foresters (an association of 620,000 members in 1910) would make members better citizens, whether their role in the outside world was humble or mighty:

> The man who has served in the Court-room knows the virtue of obedience to lawful and kindly command, and makes a better servant outside than he who obeys blindly and renders service unintelligently. The man who has exercised authority in the Court, called to the place of honour and power by the free choice of his brethren, is not the less qualified for positions of responsibility over his fellow men in the outer world, and is much less likely to exercise with haughty arrogance the authority entrusted to his hands, than he who has never been taught the responsibility of duty even in command, nor learned the noble lesson of humility in power, which is gained in the school of mutual dependence.[12]

As these words testify, the tragedy of the incorporation of the friendly societies into the state after 1911 was not only that voluntarism was thus destroyed, but also that fine institutions which had helped to mould the moral qualities of the nation were displaced.

5

Cash Benefits and Family Independence

For the typical working-class family accident, illness and death could bring great hardship. If the breadwinner died, in addition to the emotional loss, the family also had to shoulder the cost of the funeral, no light task during the nineteenth century when the bereaved were expected to put on a bit of a show.

Each man made regular contributions to a common fund. If his earning power was interrupted by illness or accident he could draw a weekly allowance, sufficient to keep himself and his family. The fund also met the cost of medical care. In the event of the death of either a man or his wife, the surviving partner was entitled to a fixed sum sufficient to pay for the funeral; and if the breadwinner died, the society would support the widow and orphans. The chief services had always been the sick pay, the medical care and the supply of medicines.

In the affiliated friendly societies, every member carried a rule book which told him what his contribution was and the benefits he was entitled to. Court *Robert Gordon* of the Ancient Order of Foresters, based in North Shields, listed its benefits on the first page of its rules:

1. Insuring certain sums of money on the lives of its members, and for the burial of members' wives, widows, or children.

2. Paying a weekly allowance to members when bodily or mentally sick, and thereby unable to follow their employment.

3. Supplying medical attendance and medicine to members.

4. Granting relief to members in distressed circumstances.

5. Assisting members when on travel in search of employment.

6. Providing through the Order pensions for members in old age.[1]

By the turn of the century new benefits were being added. For instance, maternity benefit was offered by the Foresters from 1907.[2]

Contributions and Benefits

Both contributions and benefits varied between societies. This gave prospective friendly society members considerable freedom of choice. Those who preferred to pay, or could only afford, a low contribution could find a suitable society. And those who wished to pay more could find societies with higher benefits and corresponding contribution scales. The conditions on which payment would be made and the willingness of societies to accept those with existing illnesses or disabilities also varied.

The most common practice was that of the affiliated orders, whose members paid a combined contribution for sickness and funeral benefit and, if they wished, a further sum for medical care and medicines. The usual procedure was for the member to pay the contribution at the monthly meeting, but it was permissible for a member to wait until the end of the quarter when he could pay at the 'summoned' meeting which every member was obliged to attend on pain of a fine. Every Forester, for example, received a 'summons notice' of the quarterly meeting which included a note of how much he owed.

Court *Robert Gordon*'s contributions in 1907 included an initiation fee which increased with age and for those who had joined before 1907, the regular sick and funeral fund contribution which was payable every four weeks and varied with age of joining. The initiation fees and four-weekly contributions are shown in Tables 2 and 3.

After 1907 contributions increased according to the year of joining as follows. There were three scales. The cheapest began at 1s 11½d (approx. 10p) per month for those joining at 18, increasing each year to 3s 7d (approx. 18p) for those joining at 39. The most costly scale began at 2s 4½d (approx. 12p) for 18 year-olds and increased to 4s 3d (approx. 21p) for those aged 39. In addition members paid 6d (2½p) per month to the management fund to cover the cost of administration, plus one penny a month to the subsidiary benefits fund to cover other benefits like travel and special cases of distress.

Sick pay for members before 1907 was: 10s (50p) per week for 12 weeks, 7s (35p) for 14 weeks, 5s (25p) for 26 weeks and 2s 6d (12½p) thereafter. From 1907 a higher rate was paid: £1 for the first 26 weeks, 10s for the next 26 and 5s thereafter. A funeral benefit of £10 was paid to the wife if the member died and £5 to any man who lost his wife.

Table 2

Initiation Fees, Ancient Order of Foresters, 1907

Age	Initiation Fee
18-24	2s 6d
25-29	5s 0d
30-34	7s 6d
35-39	10s 0d

Table 3

Sick and Funeral Fund Contribution, 1907
Ancient Order of Foresters

Age	Fee
18-21	1s 5d
22-25	1s 7d
26-29	1s 9d
30-34	2s 0d
35-39	2s 4d

Normally in the Foresters a member had to wait twelve months after declaring off the sick fund before he was entitled to the full rate of sick pay for the same illness. But if he contracted a different complaint during that time he was entitled to full benefit.[3] In Court *Robert Gordon*, a member had to have been off sick pay for only six months before the full rate was payable again.[4]

All told, during a twelve-month period an 18-year old on the lowest scale would have paid 30s 6d (approx. £1.52) a year and a man of 39, 50s (£2.50). For the younger man on average earnings this was the equivalent of about one week's wages a year, and for the older man about 1½ weeks. In 1906 the average wage of unskilled workers was about 22s (£1.10) a week; for the semi-skilled, about 28s (£1.40); and for the skilled worker, around 37s (£1.85) a week.[5]

Medical care was extra, costing at the turn of the century between 4s (20p) and 5s (25p) a year, as described in Chapter 7.

Claiming Sick Pay

Sickness benefit was controlled by each lodge. The most common procedure was for a member to write a note to the branch secretary saying that he was unable to work. Usually the rules of each society laid down a set form of words which had to be used. Members of the Foresters' Court *Robert Gordon* were required to write: 'Being by illness unable to attend my employment, I hereby claim the benefit of the Court from [date] according to the rules'.[6]

The members were also required to obtain a certificate from the lodge doctor verifying that they were unable to carry on working due to illness or accident. The claims were considered by the monthly branch meetings. Sick pay was not automatically paid for every sickness. Most societies, for instance, had rules which excluded indisposition due to venereal disease or drunkenness. The 1907 *General Laws* of the Ancient Order of Foresters provided that benefit is not payable if a member suffers from an injury or illness 'caused by fighting (except in his own defence), or by following any unlawful game, exercise or pursuit, or by living an immoral life'.[7]

Visiting the Sick

All the societies arranged for sick members to be visited at least once a week, except where the illness was infectious. Some societies required a visit every day. Usually a particular official was charged with the responsibility. In the Foresters the sick visitor was the woodward. Typically, the woodward was required to visit sick members 'once a week, or oftener if necessary' and to report every court night on their condition. Court *Old Abbey*, based at Guisborough in Yorkshire, required the woodward to visit once a week on Saturday before noon.[8] The regular visits provided comfort to ailing members, especially older members or brothers in hospital. Practical help, too, was provided and lodges often kept a supply of medical appliances to lend to sick members.

The sick visitors generally pursued their task religiously, often walking or cycling many miles to visit sick brothers. They ensured that sick pay was being claimed legitimately, and actually paid the sick allowance. Sick visitors were also charged with reporting back to the lodge that the rules applying to members receiving sick pay were being observed. For example, one society prohibited sick members from 'gaming, or performing any work or labour', or from consuming intoxicating drink without the surgeon's permission. It was also provided that no member on the sick list, 'Should be out of his house after seven o'clock in winter or after nine o'clock at night in summer, unless sufficient reason be given'.[9]

Sick Pay and Local Control

Local control of the sick pay was essential to the control of fraud. The Prudential Assurance Company, the largest of the industrial assurance companies, had to abandon sick pay because, as its secretary told the Royal Commission on Friendly Societies in 1873, 'after five years' experience we found we were unable to cope with the fraud that was practised'. The centralised friendly societies also found it difficult to control fraud. The Hearts of Oak Benefit Society, the largest and most efficient of the centralised societies, had no branches at all, and dispensed all benefits from its head office. Its rate of sickness was habitually far in excess of the experience of the Foresters or the Oddfellows. According to its actuary, this was due to inadequate provision against malingering. During the eight years 1884-91, for instance, the 'expected sickness,' according to the 1866-70 experience of the Manchester Unity of Oddfellows was 1,111,553 weeks; whereas the actual weeks for which benefit was drawn numbered no fewer than 1,452,106, an excess of over thirty per cent.[10]

This is a common problem which arises whenever beneficiaries no longer feel a real sense of participation. When branches administered sick pay the members knew who was paying—it was the members themselves. But if 'head office' made the payment, it was possible to entertain the illusion that someone else was bearing the cost. And the centralised insurer had no better answer to this illusion than today's government departments. Some centralised friendly societies, such as the National Deposit Friendly Society, combined saving with insurance to overcome the difficulty and in the local societies and branches of the affiliated orders, members felt they had a real stake in the organisation to an extent which proved sufficient, not only to discourage selfishness, but also to build a genuine sense of fraternity. There was some fraud, but for many members a spirit of brotherhood did guide their conduct.

Many preferred not to claim sick pay at all, however strong their entitlement. And of those who did so, the great majority only claimed their due. Nor did local self-administration inevitably mean ineffic-iency or unreliability. Those federal societies which combined branch autonomy with a central relief fund for branches which got into financial difficulties, successfully achieved both real local participation and a guaranteed standard of service.

Thus, the affiliated friendly societies handled the problem of fraud far more effectively than do today's welfare bureaucracies. Sick pay was administered by the local branch, which meant not just that effective supervision was more feasible, but also that it was possible to create a real sense of moral responsibility amongst members. Those who chose to cheat were defrauding not some faceless bureaucracy, but their own brothers. And in a very real sense, they cheated themselves, for the funds of each branch were nothing more than the contributions of each member.[11]

Sick Pay and Pensions

Special provision was often made for those who became permanently disabled. Most societies also provided convalescent homes, usually as a result of several lodges pooling their resources. London friendly societies had their own convalescent home, as did those in the Midlands and the North East, whose members paid 1s a year towards the Grange-over-Sands home.[11]

As members became older they became more susceptible to illness and men who performed more arduous jobs, found it difficult to continue working at all. Members who, through old age rather than illness, were unable to carry on working were paid sickness benefit by most societies. This put a huge strain on the funds of many lodges because the contributions had been set to cover sick pay only. The societies struggled to come up with an answer to this problem for many years. In the short run the societies sought to maintain the solvency of branches with liabilities to older members which they would be unable to meet by (a) recruiting younger members; (b) introducing higher contributions graduated according to age of joining; (c) creating a central contingency fund to support weaker branches; and (d) imposing additional levies on members from time to time. Their long-term plan was to encourage members to make additional contributions for a pension or deferred annuity.

From 1882 the two largest affiliated orders introduced pension schemes. Under the rules of the Foresters' superannuation fund a member aged 30 could pay a single premium of £20 7s 8d (approx. £20.38) for a deferred annuity of 5s (25p) per week from age 65, or an annual premium of 23s 5d (approx. £1.17) till age 65. All premiums were returnable in the event of early death.[12] But the take up was very low. For example, the Manchester Unity of Oddfellows scheme for deferred annuities introduced in 1882 had attracted by 1893 only somewhat over 500 members out of 700,000. The Foresters also found few members were interested.[13]

Travelling in Search of Work

The rules of most branches expressly provided for 'assisting members when on travel in search of employment'.[14] The system provided not only for members to travel in search of a new job but also, if successful, to transfer to the nearest local branch. In the Foresters, the member who had paid his contributions for a year was required to obtain a certificate (called a clearance) confirming that he was fully paid up. He then applied for a travelling licence and, if granted, was given at least six pre-paid cheques worth 1s 3d (approx. 6p) and told the travelling password (which was changed every quarter).[15] The member would report to the local district secretary and, if able to give the password and offer the correct handshake and knowledge of the signs of Forestry, would be able to cash one cheque each day and two on a Saturday. The licence could be valid for up to six weeks. If he found a job, the member could 'throw in' his clearance to the local branch. The usual rule was that any member of twelve months standing who was clear on the books was entitled to a transfer. However, the new branch did not have to accept him and in the rare case of refusal, the member was allowed one month to return to his own court, which was bound to receive him back.[16] Contributions were payable according to the member's original date of joining, so there was no disadvantage in transferring.[17]

In the Manchester Unity a member of twelve months duration obtained a card from his lodge secretary which showed the benefit due in sickness or death. It was valid for six months and entitled him to report to any lodge, which would then pay his travelling expenses. The lodge's costs could be reclaimed from the central funds. In some districts it had also long been the practice to provide medical care for travelling members. Under the 1840 rules of the Sheffield District of Manchester Unity, for instance, the surgeons were required to attend without additional charge members from other lodges travelling in search of work.[18]

Manchester Unity members who found it necessary to move for whatever reason, could also transfer to the nearest branch. Just as when he applied to travel in search of work, the member's old branch issued him with a 'clearance' certificate which he could 'throw in' to his new lodge. The clearance system operated internationally from early in the last century.[19] Migrants to Australia, New Zealand, Canada, or the United States of America, for instance, thus found themselves immediately among friends.

The Ancient Order of Foresters began to record clearances from 1871 and its records show that between 1871 and 1875 a little over 1,000 members a year took advantage of the system. In the Manchester Unity between 1848 and 1872 16,086 members were issued with travelling documents.[20] As the Chief Registrar of Friendly Societies said to the Royal Commission on Labour in 1892:

> The organisation of the affiliated orders therefore lends itself much more than that of the isolated friendly societies to industrial freedom and independence. The working man, who is not satisfied with his lot can leave his place of employment and seek for work elsewhere, and he gets material help while on the search, and finds friends who may give him advice.[21]

Help For The Bereaved

Court *Old Abbey* at Guisborough in the 1870s, paid £10 to the wife on the death of a member, and £5 to the husband who lost his wife.[22] But the societies did not stop at making cash payments to the surviving spouse.

In addition, the society also ensured a good turnout at the funeral. In the early years many lodges made attendance compulsory for all branch members and failure to attend would result in a fine. In the 1850s Court *Old Abbey* fined members one shilling for non-attendance.[23] In later years compulsory attendance was not a requirement and by 1907, attitudes had reversed and the Foresters' rules prohibited compulsory attendance of funerals.[24] Society ritual also played its part. The leading societies each had a funeral oration which the senior officer would recite at the graveside.

The society's concern did not end with the funeral. Members made certain that a widow and her children did not suffer. They ensured that family members had somewhere to live and that they did not go hungry. And they ensured that the children were edu-

6

Who Joined?

Candidates for membership of the sick and funeral funds had to conform to three main requirements. They had to be of the prescribed age, in good health and of good character. The age and health requirements served to ensure that everyone joined the fund on roughly equal terms. The great majority of societies admitted members at the age of 18. The Grand United Order of Oddfellows admitted members at 16, the Independent Order of Rechabites at 15, and one or two minor teetotal orders accepted members as young as 14. Few societies accepted members after the age of 40, though the United Ancient Order of Druids took members up to 45 and the Rechabites accepted members up to 50. And many societies would admit members over the prescribed age upon payment of additional contributions. In the 1850s Foresters' courts were entitled to admit members over 40 on payment of 12s 6d plus the normal annual contribution and an additional 9s for every year of age over 40.[1] By the end of the century the societies were encouraging the establishment of children's lodges. By 1907 the *General Laws* of the Foresters provided for children to become junior members between the ages of one and eighteen.

Applicants for membership of the sick and funeral fund had to pass a medical examination. The rule applied by the Foresters in 1857 was that no one in ill health could be admitted. The 1907 rule was that:

> No person shall be admitted a Member of the Order who is partially paralysed, of unsound constitution, in ill-health or who is minus a foot or hand, an arm, or a leg, or short of an eye, or who is suffering from a rupture, except as an Honourary Member.[2]

Applicants were also expected to be of 'good character'. The Foresters provided that no individual could be admitted: 'who bears a bad character, who leads a dissolute life, frequents bad company, is guilty of habitual intoxication, or is of a quarrelsome behaviour.'[3]

The usual procedure in the affiliated societies was for candidates' names to be announced at the end of one monthly meeting and considered at the next. Each candidate required a proposer who could testify to their good character and who was expected not to take his testimony lightly. In the Manchester Unity in 1867 every lodge in the vicinity received a notice of persons being proposed, and anyone knowing anything for or against the candidate was requested to attend.[4]

These were the formal rules. But during the last century, when many people had no birth certificate, enforcement of the age limit was much more difficult than it is today. And anyway, some lodges were keen to recruit and did not enforce the age-limit strictly. Neither was the health requirement as strictly enforced as a cursory reading of the rules might suggest.

But, during the last century, even where the rule was strictly applied it only affected membership of the sick and funeral fund. For those not permitted to join that fund there remained the possibility of becoming an honourary member, with the right to medical benefit. The Foresters permitted any 'respectable person' to become an honourary member by paying an entrance fee of 10s 6d (52½p).[5] Honourary members were permitted to express an opinion on all questions brought before their court, but had no vote. More importantly, they could avail themselves of the services of the court surgeon, for which they paid 50 per cent more than financial members.

What did the requirement that a person be of 'good character' mean in practice? Rule 77 of the Foresters' 1857 *General Laws* provides for criminals to be expelled and for the suspension of members found guilty of attempting to 'defraud another Brother of what is justly his due'. In such a case 'he shall be suspended until he make restitution and evince by his actions that he is brought to a sense of shame and sorrow for his fault'. Thus, the intention of the rules was to mould good character and to promote reform where fault was found. Under Rule 40 of the Foresters' 1907 *General Laws*, a member convicted of a criminal offence could be expelled by a vote of his local branch. However, if he lived 'a sober, honest and virtuous life' for a year and showed sincere repentance he could be re-admitted, but a second offence would mean expulsion for life.

This seems to have been characteristic of other societies. Few candidates were rejected at all, and of those who were, the most important reason for their rejection was criminal or shady conduct in their immediate past. Occasionally members were expelled. This too was usually the result of criminal conduct, although sometimes a member was expelled for a moral failure such as deserting his wife and children.

Membership of the Friendly Societies for Sick Pay

Membership figures for registered friendly societies were published annually by the Registrar of Friendly Societies. But in some years the total figure includes 'collecting societies', which were more like industrial assurance companies than friendly societies proper and invariably offered only a death benefit. To arrive at the membership of friendly societies offering the main services of sick pay and funeral benefit, the membership of the collecting societies has to be deducted.

After adjustment downwards to exclude the collecting societies the official figure requires adjustment upwards to take into account members of unregistered friendly societies. The Royal Commission on the Friendly Societies of 1874 reported, after searching inquiry, that the extent of unregistered was as large as that of registered societies. But did this continue to be the case over the next forty years or so? Sir Edward Brabrook, the Chief Registrar of Friendly Societies, testified to the Royal Commission on Labour in 1892 that the ratio of registered to unregistered members was still about the same. There were 3.8 million registered friendly society members out of an industrial male population of seven million. Allowing for double membership this represented at least three million individuals in registered societies, and assuming a similar number of unregistered members there were at least six million members in total. In addition, Brabrook felt that some trade union members should also be added to the total, for some trade unions also offered friendly benefits. And we know that trade unions were in competition with the friendly societies for members, at least to some extent.[6] In 1893 there were about 870,000 registered trade union members. Some of these should be added to Brabrook's six million. Brabrook concluded:

> It would look as if there was really merely a kind of residuum left of those who are in uncertain work or otherwise, and are not able to insure in some shape or other.[7]

He confirmed his view two years later before the Royal Commission on the Aged Poor. A member of his staff had recently visited Norfolk and found many unregistered societies. In many cases some old registered societies of a hundred years standing or more had been replaced by unregistered societies: 'So I think it beyond doubt that the sphere of unregistered societies is exceedingly large'.[8]

Was Brabrook's assumption still valid on the eve of national insurance? He gave evidence to the Royal Commission on the Poor Laws in 1906 and confirmed his view that registered and unregistered membership were about equal.[9] Moreover, useful evidence was presented to the Royal Commission on the Poor Laws by A.C. Kay and H.V. Toynbee. They carried out a major investigation of voluntary provision for the poor in several towns and rural areas and found considerable unregistered activity. They studied three large towns (Norwich, York, and Coventry), two moderate-sized towns (Beverley and Kendal), three small towns (Ludlow, Lichfield, and Bourne), and five rural districts. Brabrook had referred to the 'growing popularity' of slate clubs,[10] and Kay and Toynbee certainly found a large number of unregistered dividing societies in the areas they investigated. They found that dividing societies were commonly attached to public houses and workplaces in York, Norwich and Coventry. There was an especially large one at Coleman's in Norwich, and 'nearly all' the Coventry factories had dividing societies. In York they were attached to the Adult Schools. Some were attached to churches, but to a far smaller extent than they believed to have been the case in earlier years.[11]

Beveridge, in *Voluntary Action* published in 1948, estimated that about five million of the 12 million originally included in the national insurance scheme were already members of friendly societies offering sick pay.[12] But his figure does not include unregistered friendly societies and we know from the Registrar himself, as well as the Royal Commission on the Poor Laws, that unregistered membership was similar to registered. If that assumption is valid, then three quarters or more of the 12 million must have already been covered by voluntary provision of some kind.

Did the Poor Join Friendly Societies?

Rowntree found in York in 1901 that the '*very poor* are but seldom members of Friendly Societies', and he commented that, 'Even if they can be induced to join, they soon allow their membership to lapse'.[13] Was this generally true, and was it because the friendly societies catered only for the well-paid workers? Professor Bentley Gilbert writes, for example, that the friendly societies 'made no appeal whatever to the grey, faceless, lower third of the working-classes'. Friendly society membership was, he said 'the badge of the skilled worker'. It was not for the 'crossing sweeper, the dock labourer, the railroad navvy, any more that it was for the landowner, the member of Parliament, or the company director'.[14]

Many dock workers were in shop (works) clubs run by the dock companies, usually on dividing principles. But some were also in the permanent friendly societies. This was demonstrated in 1898 when the London and East India Docks Company tried to forbid employees from being members of outside societies. The company had organised its own Docks Friendly Society to pay sick pay and had found that men who belonged to an outside friendly society as well as to the company society had an inducement to stay off work, because the company sick pay plus the outside sick pay came to more than their normal wage. When membership of outside friendly societies was banned, Manchester Unity and the other large societies campaigned vigorously against the decision. They pressed parliament for legislation to forbid companies from restricting their employees' freedom of choice in this manner, arguing that there was a parallel with 'truck', the system of payment in kind.[15]

This shows two things. First that there were some dock workers in the affiliated friendly societies, certainly enough to alarm their leaders when the company forced its employees to leave. Secondly, it shows that the friendly societies were keen to recruit from among dock workers. So if the dockers did not join, it was not the doing of the large friendly societies. Testimony to the Royal Commission on the Poor Laws also tends to contradict Gilbert. The Royal Commission was told that among the 4,000 Manchester Unity members in Liverpool were a 'good many' earning irregular wages averaging less than 25s a week. Many of these were dock workers, but generally the Royal Commission was told that dock workers belonged to their own dividing societies.[16] Finally, evidence from Huddersfield suggests that low-paid railway labourers joined the major friendly societies in large numbers. A Huddersfield poor law guardian who was also a member of the Ancient Order of Foresters, testified that a 'large majority' of local members were unskilled labourers such as railway labourers earning 18s a week. Indeed, the 'vast majority' of railwaymen, including the lowest paid, joined both friendly societies and trade unions. Some earned even less, but most unskilled workers in Huddersfield earned from 18s to 22s 6d a week.[17] Manchester Unity members' wage rates were also reported to start from the 18s mark, rising to 28s a week.[18]

Kay and Toynbee's investigation for the Royal Commission on the Poor Laws revealed that in the three large towns they studied wage rates were lowest in Norwich, with skilled workers earning from 18s to 23s. Yet in Norwich, friendly society membership was much higher than in the other towns. Local friendly society leaders told the investigators that this was *because* wages were low: the lower paid had to think more carefully about how to provide for themselves in the event of sickness. Better paid workers had more alternatives available.[19] The investigators found this surprising and pursued the issue further. Generally they found that registered friendly society membership was highest in rural areas where wages were lowest. They reproduced a table which had been published by the Ancient Order of Foresters (the second largest society) comparing its membership in 1902 with county populations in 1901. Rural counties scored highest, and industrialised ones lowest.

The Norfolk figure of 61 per 1000 was the highest, and Lancashire, a highly industrialised county, was lowest with four.[20] Other evidence from industrialised Coventry suggested that when workers earned higher wages they tended to become more interested in saving and somewhat less in protection against sickness. Some may have switched to unregistered dividing and deposit societies.[21]

The investigators were not the only ones to be surprised by the figures. J.L. Stead, the permanent secretary of the Foresters, said he had initially been surprised to learn that some of their best branches were in areas with the lowest wages and that they were relatively weaker in the larger towns where wages were high.[22] He thought that the membership of the other permanent friendly societies was similar, and expressed his pride in the fact that they had low-paid members:

> We have got some of the humblest men in the country in our society, and we are just as proud of them as of the others.[23]

Other evidence confirms that many workers on low wages joined the leading friendly societies. Claverhouse Graham, president of the Old Age State Pension League, a director of Manchester Unity since 1890, and an advocate of state pensions, told a select committee of the House of Commons that the friendly societies did not only recruit the highest paid workers. In the Eastern counties agricultural labourers on 14s to 15s a week were members. And he reckoned the average wage of members of all the societies was not one pound a week, at a time when the national average was much more.[24]

There was quite a large turnover of friendly society members but, according to the Foresters in Huddersfield, those that tended to come and go were in the eighteen to thirty age group.[25] This was also the view of the Chief Registrar of Friendly Societies.[26] But many of those who joined, left, and rejoined were receiving low wages, or were affected by the trade cycle. In Sheffield, for instance, the Royal Commission was told that men who could not keep up their contributions eventually joined the dividing societies.[27]

To sum up: a precise estimate of the number of persons on low incomes who joined friendly societies can not be made, and we are forced to rely on the testimony of contemporary observers. From this evidence it can reasonably be inferred that a considerable number of poor persons did join friendly societies, including the large national federations. Many others did not join but there is no indication that the friendly societies actively deterred the poor from joining—indeed, they were proud to have them. But there were many who ranked among the low paid, and particularly those in irregular or seasonal work, who found it difficult to keep up the contributions.

7

Medical Care

Medical care was being provided in a variety of ways at the turn of the century.[1] The very poor relied on the Poor Law, and provision for the majority of the population fell into three main categories. First, many sought medical care as private patients and paid a fee to the doctor of their choice. The fees charged varied according to income, with rent taken as the chief test of ability to pay. Second, a large section of the population obtained care free of charge through charities, such as the outpatient departments of the voluntary hospitals or free dispensaries. And third there were many pre-payment schemes, commonly called contract practice, based on the payment of a fixed annual capitation fee.

Private Fees

The fourteen-strong majority of the Royal Commission on the Poor Laws found that there were 'many', including some from the 'poorest working class' who paid fees as private patients in preference to joining clubs.[2] The Royal Commission had been told by the medical officer of health in Manchester that a 'very considerable' number of persons earning less than 30 shillings a week paid ordinary fees.[3] And there is evidence that this had been so for many years. According to the *Association Medical Journal*, in 1853 'many' workers receiving only 12s to 15s a week paid the customary private fee.[4] This is not as surprising as it may seem, for doctors charged patients according to income, and the lowest fee was within the grasp of the low-paid worker. Rent was usually taken as a rough indicator of income.

An official tariff in *Whitaker's Almanack* for 1900 distinguished three scales: those paying rents from £10 to £25 a year; those paying £25 to £50; and those paying £50 to £100 plus. The minimum fee for a surgery consultation for the poorest class was 2s 6d.[5] In fact fees actually charged were much lower. In 1889 the fee for a surgery consultation varied from 1s 0d to 2s 6d. And for a home visit (including medicine) fees varied from 1s 6d to 3s 6d. The most common fees were 2s 0d or 2s 6d, with 1s 6d charged for the very poor.[6] On the eve of National Insurance fees had, if anything, fallen slightly. In working-class areas it was 'difficult' to charge even 1s 0d per consultation, and among the 'better classes' difficult to charge as much as 3s 6d.[7]

Such fees, as long as they had to be paid only occasionally, were within the means of wage earners. In 1906 the average wage of unskilled workers was about 22s a week; for the semi-skilled, about 28s; and for the skilled worker, around 37s a week.[8] In addition, in some large manufacturing towns arrangements were sometimes made to pay fees by instalments.[9]

In addition, according to the government's survey of 1910, many people turned to unqualified medical practitioners. In eighty-two out of 217 towns studied, unqualified medical practice was either increasing or taking place in large amount, and in a further seventy-five it existed to some extent. In twenty-seven there was very little, and in thirty none. Included in the survey were chemists who prescribed over the counter, herbalists, and bonesetters, Christian scientists, faith healers, abortionists, and VD specialists. In mining areas such as Northumberland, Durham and Wales bonesetters enjoyed equal standing with doctors.[10]

Free Care

Many poor people sought care from the voluntary hospitals and charitable dispensaries, which in most large towns provided advice and medicine free to those on low incomes. At the Newcastle upon Tyne free dispensary, for instance, patients with a subscriber's letter of recommendation received attendance and medicine free, whilst 'casuals' paid 2d for any medicine prescribed.[11]

Of greatest importance for the supply of free medical care were the outpatient departments of the voluntary hospitals. *Burdett's Hospitals and Charities* (1907) estimated that one in four of the population of London obtained free medical relief in 1877, one in two and a half in 1894, and one in 2.1 in 1904. In 1887, for example, when the population of London was just over four million, there were one and a half million outpatient attendances at London hospitals. In the same year there were also 162,000 consultations at twenty-six free dispensaries; 102,000 at part-pay dispensaries; and 126,000 at provident dispensaries run on benefit society principles for the whole family.[12] Using figures published by the Hospital Sunday Fund, Arthur Newsholme (later Sir Arthur) estimated the proportion of the metropolitan population obtaining free medical care in 1907 at one in four.[13]

Outpatient departments were important in the great majority of large towns, but the London figures are not typical of the country as a whole because of the heavy concentration of hospitals in the capital. Provincial figures varied. In Newcastle in 1894 the figure was one in 1.8, in Edinburgh one in 2.7, in Glasgow one in 4.9, in Cardiff one in 7.3, and in Portsmouth one in 14.3. In Leicester in 1907, for instance, when the population was around 125,000, the General Infirmary attended 39,994 outpatients, 13,836 casualties, and admitted 2,950 inpatients.[14]

Types of Contract Practice

The various types of scheme are identified in a report of the medico-political committee of the BMA, published in 1905.[15] Each type of contract practice was based on the principle of the flat-rate annual contribution, usually payable quarterly but sometimes weekly or fortnightly, entitling the contributor to any number of consultations during the period covered. Some such clubs were based at factories, others were organised by charities; some were run on commercial lines, some by individual doctors, some by local associations of doctors, and some by the friendly societies. By far the most important numerically were the friendly society schemes.

Works Clubs (Medical Aid Societies)

A number of doctors were employed by works clubs. Workers at a factory or mine arranged with their employer to deduct an agreed sum from their pay for the provision of medical attendance and medicines for themselves, and usually for their families. Some doctors were paid a fixed salary, others an annual amount per patient. In some cases the employer himself engaged a medical practitioner to attend his workers but by the turn of the century it was more usual for the general body of employees at a factory or mine, or working in a particular district, to choose their medical attendant in a general meeting and elect a committee to manage the scheme. The most resilient of the works clubs were the 'medical aid societies' founded by the miners and steelworkers of the Welsh valleys.

Provident Dispensaries

The provident dispensaries were charities, funded partly by the contributions of beneficiaries and partly by the charitable donations of the (non-benefiting) honourary members. Provident or self-supporting dispensaries were often founded as alternatives to the free dispensaries, many of which had been established during the course of the eighteenth century. Free dispensaries were felt to create a permanently dependent section of the population and the provident dispensaries aimed to enable the poor to make as much of a contribution as they could afford to the cost of their medical care.

It was felt that the beneficiaries would feel greater self respect if they were able to pay at least something towards their own health care. They therefore paid a low annual contribution, felt to be within the means of the very poor, and the balance was supplied by the honourary members. The BMA acknowledged that many of those in provident dispensaries, private clubs, public medical services, and medical societies were 'so poor' that they were unable to pay private fees at working-class rates.[16] One of the strongest provident dispensaries was the Leicester Provident Dispensary. It had 50,798 members in 1907 and ran a small maternity home and cottage hospital. Fees were a penny a week for adults, half for children; or threepence halfpenny a week for a man, wife and all children under fourteen.[17]

Medical Aid Companies

Some contract medical practice was organised on commercial lines. The National Medical Aid Company, for instance, offered medical attendance as an inducement to obtain life-assurance business.[18] Such companies differed from the friendly societies and works clubs, which had been founded for the benefit of members and their dependants, and the promoters had little in common with the honourary members of provident dispensaries.

However, the insurance companies were a valued alternative for the poor. Usually a candidate for life assurance was required to pass a medical examination, but there was provision for those persons contributing for a very small sum assured to be admitted without medical examination at the discretion of the agent. The agents, who received a percentage of the premium income collected, had a strong financial incentive to admit such contributors, and by this method individuals who would have failed a friendly society or other medical examination were able to obtain the services of a doctor.[19] By 1905, however, the role of the insurance companies was being reduced due to pressure exerted through the General Medical Council.[20] A district medical officer in Birmingham told the Royal Commission on the Poor Laws that before the GMC's advertising and canvassing bans were imposed in 1901 and 1902 there had been a great many commercial clubs. Because of the GMC rulings these had been driven out of existence.[21]

Doctors' Clubs

There were also a large number of clubs organised by the doctors themselves. Many employed collectors to recruit new members as well as to call regularly for patients' contributions. The collector's commission was occasionally as low as 5 per cent but sometimes reached 25 per cent. Many medical practitioners criticised the doctors' clubs. One described the 'penny a week club' as 'the curse of the medical profession'. However, the BMA's survey revealed that many doctors were supportive:

> The family club run by the doctor himself is a necessity. He can be dismissed at a moment's notice very often from a Friendly Society. The individual member of his own club, if he has a complaint to make, does it personally. The doctor is free from the supervision, and, as I have found, the impertinence of the committee of the Friendly Society. The patients in a family club look up to him personally. In the Friendly Society club he is very often treated as a servant. The smallest infringement of their rules means a complaint and a visit from the committee. The doctor of a family club can make his own terms.[22]

Public Medical Services

Public medical services were rather like medical aid societies, but while the latter were controlled by lay committees, public medical services were 'under the entire control of the medical profession', as the BMA approvingly put it. In 1905 public medical services were a recent phenomenon. Usually they had been founded by the local branch of the BMA to combat provident dispensaries, medical aid societies, or friendly societies.[23]

The Friendly Society Schemes

Among the great variety of arrangements made by the friendly societies for the supply of medical care three proved most popular: the lodge system, medical institutes and approved panels.

Lodge Practice: The traditional system in the large federations was for each branch to employ a single medical officer. Usually the appointment was made by a free vote of all the members present at a general meeting. Sometimes doctors were invited to submit tenders before the election. In some areas several medical officers were appointed to a branch or a combination of branches, and the members then enjoyed a free choice among the available doctors. Sometimes medical officers were appointed at the pleasure of the branch, and sometimes for a fixed period of three months, six months, or a year.

The medical officer's duties were threefold. First, he would examine candidates for lodge membership. Second, he would examine members who were sick to determine whether or not they should receive sick pay. And third, he would provide medical attendance and medicines for each lodge member in return for a fixed annual capitation fee, usually payable by quarterly instalments.

Medical Institutes: From about 1869 a movement developed to found medical institutes to employ full-time medical officers serving the whole family. Groups of lodges banded together, raised funds and purchased or rented premises. Organisation was under the control of a committee of delegates which appointed one or more full-time medical officers, who usually received a fixed salary plus free accommodation. The medical officers' duties usually included general medical and surgical attendance, but not the dispensing of medicines. Dispensing was carried out by the medical institute's own dispenser to ensure use of the highest quality drugs.

Approved panels: By the turn of the century the closed-panel system, under which the friendly societies appointed doctors to an approved list, was growing in popularity. To be eligible to join the panel, doctors were required to observe the conditions laid down by the friendly society and particularly to accept prescribed fees. The most sophisticated scheme was that of the centralised National Deposit Friendly Society.

Medical Care on the Eve of National Insurance

How had the various types of medical service evolved in the years leading up to state intervention in 1911? A constant feature of friendly society medical care was conflict with the organised medical profession. The friendly societies represented the consumer and sought through competition to improve the quality of medical care and to contain pressure for fee increases. As the nineteenth century progressed the medical profession organised itself with ever-growing determination to eliminate competition by whatever means were available. Not all doctors, however, shared the aspirations of the BMA, the doctors' trade union, and many worked in close harmony with the friendly societies.

Early Professional Action

The medical journals began to carry references to disputes between doctors and friendly societies from the 1830s, and by the 1840s and 50s doctors began to take more concerted action. At that time the organised medical profession was not opposed to clubs as such, but doctors did seek 'considerable and immediate reform'. They had two main complaints: (1) that they were underpaid, and (2) that the friendly societies admitted members who could afford to pay higher fees.[24] By 1869 the leading medical journal, The Lancet, was referring to the 'battle of the clubs', declaring it to be 'undecided'.[25] In that year, doctors in the West Bromwich area applied to thirty-four societies for an increase in the prevailing rate of 3s (15p) per year. In a response which was probably fairly typical, eighteen of these societies increased their fees to 4s (20p); seven to 5s (25p); and in one case a new club was formed and paid 10s (50p). Nine clubs refused to respond at all. One club initially increased its rate to 4s, but a little later in June 1871, two doctors offered themselves at 3s and were appointed at the lower fee. Generally doctors felt that their agitation had been successful.[26]

The campaigns of the late 1860s and the 1870s were not characterised by the bitterness typical of later years. The Lancet found that many increases to 5s a year and more had been awarded 'without any undignified pressure, but from reasonable and courteous representations'.[27]

The Rise of the Medical Institutes

One side-effect of the doctors' agitation was the foundation of friendly society medical institutes. The first of these was opened in Preston in 1870 in response to the local doctors' campaign for an increase in fees. The doctors were pressing for a 50 per cent increase to a minimum of

3s (15p) per annum, plus an additional mileage allowance for patients who lived outside the borough. In December 1869 the Preston friendly societies had met to consider their response to the demands of what they called the 'Preston Medical Trades Union'. The result was the foundation of the Preston Associated Friendly Societies' Provident Dispensary.[28]

The immediate cause of the foundation of the medical institutes was the campaign of the doctors for increased fees. The underlying reason was not a wish to avoid paying more for medical care, but rather a sense of dissatisfaction with traditional lodge practice. There were three main criticisms. First, lodge doctors were usually part-time, serving not only other friendly society branches but also taking private patients on a fee-for-service basis. Some friendly society members in certain localities felt that their lodge medical officers were more interested in building up a lucrative private practice than in serving lodge members. To secure the undivided attention of the doctor, the friendly society medical institutes employed full-time salaried medical officers who were forbidden to take private patients.

The second criticism was that whilst some doctors would *prescribe* very expensive medicines, they would seldom *supply* them, preferring to advise the patient to pay extra at the chemists. Such doctors argued that the fixed annual capitation fee did not cover unusually expensive medicines. This practice was not universal, but it did happen. The medical institutes overcame it by buying their own drugs at wholesale prices and supplying them direct in their own dispensaries. Moreover, medical institutes would also supply nutritional items such as cod liver oil and malt.

The third criticism was that lodge practice did not usually provide for dependants. The medical institutes, therefore, provided for the whole family and not only the club member. In the 1870s most institutes charged 8s (40p) per year for the whole family, compared with 3s 6d (17½p) or 4s (20p) in lodge practice for the man only. Perinatal care was available at the concessional rate of 10s 6d (52½p). In addition, widows and orphans were allowed to continue their membership, and in some cases orphans were attended free of charge until they reached working age.

By 1877 efforts were being made to establish medical institutes, or medical aid associations, throughout England. They had been founded in Preston, Newport, Derby, Worcester, Nottingham, Bradford and elsewhere.[29] For some friendly society leaders the foundation of the medical institutes was another step in the great friendly society crusade, summed up in a phrase subsequently purloined by the welfare state: to provide for members from 'the cradle to the grave'. Leaders of the movement, it was said, would not consider their work complete until this had been achieved.[30]

In 1879 the Friendly Societies Medical Alliance (FSMA) had been established to promote the common interests of friendly society medical institutes. By 1882 the FSMA had established a medical agency (a kind of labour exchange) at which doctors deposited their names and qualifications and to which medical institutes turned when they needed a doctor.[31] In 1883, thirty-two medical institutes with a total of 139,000 members sent full returns to the FSMA. There were institutes in Bradford, Birmingham, Bristol, Derby, Exeter, Greenock, Hull, Hartlepool, Leeds, Leicester, Lincoln, Lowestoft, Newport, Northampton, Portsmouth, Reading, Sheffield, West Bromwich, Wolverhampton and elsewhere. The largest was at York, with 9,300 members.[32]

In 1898 there were about forty medical institutes registered as friendly societies with around 213,000 members, employing about seventy-five medical officers. In addition there were unregistered medical institutes. In 1896 there were at least five with around 19,000 members.[33] At least twenty owned their own premises, combining surgery, dispensary, and doctor's living accommodation. Annual capitation fees varied, but were usually 3s for men, 4s to 5s for wives, and 1s for children. In some cases an inclusive fee for the whole family was charged, varying from 3s 6d to around 8s 0d. The fee for peri-natal care remained at 10s 6d. The largest institute was at Derby with 11,600 members. York was the second largest with 10,300 members, followed by Wolverhampton with 8,700.

The Battle of the Clubs

Several leading academic studies of the period have placed too much reliance on the doctors' version of events. Professor Bentley Gilbert, for example, cites the assertion of Alfred Cox, the medical secretary of the BMA, that 'it was no secret that many of the appointments were obtained by bribery and corruption'. And Gilbert continues, 'jobs were auctioned off to the lowest bidder'.[34] The reality was more complex, and at the turn of the century doctors' combinations to raise fees met a variety of responses.

The experience of the Portsmouth Medical Union was probably typical. In addition to seeking pay increases from friendly societies, medical aid societies and Poor Law Guardians, the Portsmouth Medical Union set out to maintain a 'patients black list' and to prevent the extension of contract practice to women.[35] Their campaign for higher fees met a mixed response. The two medical officers of the Portsmouth Medical Benefit Society, a society run by dockyard workers and funded by pay-packet deductions, resigned in protest at the low fees. The dock workers found other doctors to fill their places. However, some dock workers sympathised with the original medical officers and established a new benefit society which offered them more favourable terms.[36] A couple of months later, in November 1895, one of Portsmouth's largest Oddfellows lodges held an election for its medical officer. The existing medical officer, Dr Lord, was refusing to accept the new terms on offer, especially the children's rate of 2s 6d per annum. Dr Lord demanded 4s. Three outside competitors stood against him, much to the annoyance of the *British Medical Journal (BMJ)*. One offered to attend juveniles at 2s 6d, one at 2s and another at 1s 6d. In the event Dr Lord was so well respected that he was decisively re-elected at his higher fee, having won 168 votes against 65, 31 and 11 for his opponents.[37]

In the 1890s the campaigns against the clubs had begun to be more effectively organised. By 1895 *The Lancet* had appointed a special commissioner to report on 'the battle of the clubs' and by December 1896, thirty-seven reports had been published. From 1895 the *BMJ* index carried regular references to the battle of the clubs. By 1896 calls were being made to adopt an openly trade union stance and some doctors were condemning their less militant colleagues as 'blacklegs'.[38] But notwithstanding the increased organisation and increased militancy of the profession, doctors' attempts to establish monopolies continued to fail. Professional efforts to raise fees met a range of responses, and capitation fees increased steadily towards 4s or 5s. But whenever a professional combination was faced with determined opposition from the friendly societies, the doctors were defeated.

Abusing the Power of the State

Some doctors grew frustrated with their partial failure and began to argue that trade combination was inadequate to the task. They urged their colleagues to make more vigorous use of the powers of the General Medical Council (GMC) to overcome the dominant consumer. The chief attraction of the GMC was that under the 1858 Medical Act, it had the power to remove doctors from the Medical Register if they were guilty of 'infamous conduct in any professional respect'. Removal meant the end of a doctor's career.

Some doctors took the view that it constituted 'infamous conduct' to fail to cooperate with professional restrictive practices intended to limit competition and raise fees. These doctors tried to use the GMC to get other colleagues struck off the Medical Register for failing to take part in trade disputes. These moves began in earnest in 1892.

The approach to the GMC was led by the Medical Defence Union (MDU) which concentrated its attack on medical aid associations, a term which included commercial organisations as well as friendly society medical institutes. The MDU claimed that medical aid association doctors were 'sweated' for the profit of the associations. The GMC's response was to appoint a committee which reported in June 1893. The criticisms of the MDU were answered by a doctor serving as the medical officer of a friendly society medical institute. He refuted the view that medical officers were 'sweated', and argued that, on the contrary, they had taken positions as medical officers to escape previous sweating practised on them by private medical practitioners who had employed them as assistants. Speaking on behalf of all his fellow medical officers, he reported that they had previously been required to work harder for less pay as assistants to fellow doctors. Most had been given workloads at least twice as heavy while they were assistants, and some had carried burdens three times as great. Indeed, this was a long-standing grievance.[39] He denied that the friendly societies made profits from their work. If there was a surplus, as there occasionally was, it was re-invested to provide security of incomes in the future: 'We were quite satisfied that our income should be thus secured, and we do not lay claim to this money'.[40]

The GMC committee was conscious of the differences between friendly society medical institutes and the commercial organisations and commented that in presenting its report committee members 'desired to show great deference to the legitimate and beneficial work of the friendly societies'.[41] The committee demonstrated its confidence in the Friendly Societies Medical Alliance by recommending that all medical institutes should conform to its Guide-Rules.[42]

The rules laid down that 2,000–2,500 patients required one full-time medical officer; 2,500–3,500 required one medical officer plus a full-time dispenser; 3,500–4,500 required a senior medical officer plus an assistant medical officer; and more than 4,500 required either three medical officers, or two plus a full-time dispenser. According to the GMC committee, however, these limits were 'often exceeded'.

The Medical Defence Union, which had initiated the complaint, demanded that service in a medical institute be declared infamous conduct, except where an appointment was on ordinary club terms.[43] The committee did not agree. The GMC concluded that the investigation by their committee had not disclosed the prevalence of any offences within the statutory province of the Council.[44]

By the 1890s pay and conditions in the medical institutes varied, but the lowest rate of pay seems to have been £120 per year for the most junior appointments. On top of this there was usually free accommodation plus heating and travel allowances. Senior medical officers usually received in excess of £200, and the best commanded well over £300. There were plenty of applicants for vacancies, even at the lowest salaries. For example, in 1893 there were seventy-five applicants for one position at a salary of £120, plus a house.[45] This was because many established doctors in private practice were employing doctors as assistants for far less, often at between £60 and £80 a year.

Pressure on the General Medical Council was maintained. Some doctors were openly arguing for it to be used to enforce specific rates of pay. One doctor, for example, complained of the 'beggarly pittance' which contract practice afforded, and called on the GMC to rule it 'infamous conduct' to accept less than a minimum fee.[46] At times, to the regret of some of its members, meetings of the GMC resembled discussions of trade-union tactics.[47] Pressure on the GMC continued and in November 1901, in a major turning point, 'canvassing' was held to be infamous conduct. And a year later came a second equally important decision, that advertising was also infamous conduct.

Capturing the State—the Effects on Professional Power

The decisions of 1901 and 1902 were the first occasions on which the powers of the GMC had been openly used to further the pecuniary interests of doctors at the expense of patients. The significance of these decisions was well understood at the time. The decision against canvassing aroused much press interest, and accusations that the GMC had become an instrument of 'trade-unionism' were common. Hitherto the majority of doctors on the GMC had honourably refused to abuse the power of the state for sectional ends. As E.M. Little, the BMA's historian, was to comment: the profession now found weapons 'placed in its hands which it did not fail to use with effect'.[48] Competition, with all its advantages for the consumer, was no longer only something which might upset colleagues—it might now lead to the loss of a doctor's livelihood. The BMA rammed home this message in the *British Medical Journal*. In 1903 the *BMJ* published a series of accounts of successful campaigns which had been conducted up and down the country, including actions in Durham, Gateshead, Walsall and Rotherham.[49]

Competition can only work if there is a free flow of information to the consumer. Canvassing and advertising are two of the chief ways in which information enabling the consumer to differentiate between producers is made available. It is, perhaps, no coincidence that canvassing went first, for the advertiser simply places new information about price or quality before the consumer, whereas the canvasser actively draws the consumer's attention to the merits of the proffered service. Both activities protect the consumer's interests; and both were effectively outlawed by the GMC after 1902.

What difference did the canvassing and advertising rulings make to professional power? In 1905 the BMA published a major investigation of contract practice, carried out by its medico-political committee which had circularised 12,000 doctors and received replies from 1,548. Of these, 692 were not engaged in contract practice and 856 were. Of those who answered the question about pay rates, 458 replied that their own rates were too low, and 165 that they were satisfied. Rates of pay among doctors serving friendly societies or similar clubs varied a good deal according to the 1,641 cases reported to the BMA inquiry. As Table 4 shows, about a quarter of clubs were paying less than 4s, and about three quarters 4s or more. About a quarter paid 5s or more.

The most common figures were 4s 0d or 4s 4d. This was due to the convenience of collecting a penny a week. Most large friendly societies paid the whole 4s 4d direct to the doctor. In the Ancient Order of Foresters, for instance, the whole of the medical contribution was paid direct to the doctor, with only the 'odd exception'.[50] But it was common for some of the smaller societies to pay the doctor 4s 0d, retaining 4d for the cost of administration. This was very cheap compared with doctors' private clubs. Usually doctors paid their collectors from 10 to 25 per cent of the fee.[51]

Table 4
Doctors' Pay in Contract Practice, 1905

Rate of Pay	Proportion of Doctors
2s and under 3s	8%
3s and under 4s	16%
4s and under 5s	53%
5s and over	24%

The survey relied on voluntary responses and it is, therefore, not unreasonable to suppose that the findings were weighted in favour of dissatisfied doctors. If so, the medical profession did not have very much to complain about. Of the 458 doctors who said their rates were too low, 393 suggested the rates that would satisfy them. About 70 per cent of them proposed rates between 4s and 6s per year, and just under half would have been satisfied with 5s or less. These aspirations were gradually being met.

The friendly societies emphasised the practical attractions of contract practice, of which many doctors were only too keenly aware. As the Chief Registrar of Friendly Societies reported in 1901, the friendly societies desired to pay a fair price for their medical service. They were 'neither beggars nor sweaters'. As one leading article in the *Oddfellows Magazine* saw it, contract practice was simply good business. It was no more than good commercial practice to discount ordinary fees in return for a regular income, freedom from book-keeping and from the risk of bad debts. The lodge secretary did after all take over some of the administrative functions which would otherwise have had to be undertaken by the doctor or a secretary.[52] The doctor's income came regularly, and it was collected either without any charge or for a trifling sum compared with the cost of employing collectors.

Moreover, the lodges cooperated with doctors in keeping costs to a minimum. It was customary, for example, for all medicine bottles to be returned to the doctor. Failure to return a bottle would result in having to pay for it. And the friendly societies tried to encourage members not to make unreasonable demands for home visits.[53]

The canvassing and advertising bans seem to have had little impact on the expansion of the medical institutes. They continued to prosper. In England alone in 1910, the last year before national insurance, medical institutes reached the peak of their influence. In that year there were eighty-five medical institutes registered as friendly societies, with 329,450 members. Assuming (based on 1896 figures) that unregistered societies comprised around 13 per cent of the total there would have been (as suggested by the only contemporary estimate) about a hundred institutes in 1912, with a membership of approximately 350,000. About thirty of the medical institutes owned their own surgeries and dispensaries.[54]

Doctors' Fondness for Hyperbole

In February 1909 a meeting between representatives of the friendly societies and the BMA was held under the aegis of the Charity Organisation Society. A reasonably friendly exchange of views took place, but no agreement was reached on a wage limit, the doctors' chief concern. Friendly societies steadfastly refused to recruit only those who earned less than a certain wage. At these meetings some doctors demonstrated their fondness for hyperbole. At the February 1909 meeting, Sir Thomas Barlow said that the life of the club doctor was one of 'absolute slavery', and that he would rather cut off his right hand than become a club doctor. A friendly society delegate pointed out that this might be true of some doctors, but he cited the case of another who had sold his contract practice for £100. Some doctors, he commented wryly, were so opposed to lodge practice that they insisted on putting a high price on it.[55] Nor was it uncommon for doctors to buy and sell the contract side of a practice. As the former grand master of Manchester Unity, told a packed meeting of friendly society delegates in the Albert Hall in 1911, one doctor had lately paid a sum of five times the annual value of his contract practice: 'A very astonishing thing it is', said the friendly society leader, 'that these doctors are so innocent, so unsuspecting, so unbusinesslike, such children in these things that they pay five years purchase for that which is not worth having'.[56]

To sum up: during the 80 or so years before the 1911 National Insurance Act the organised consumer was usually more powerful than the organised producer, and in a few localities at least, a situation, not of monopoly, but of monopsony existed. Doctors could not unilaterally determine fees (though fees were rising by the consent of both parties); they could not impose an income limit to exclude the well-paid; and they could not stop the establishment and growth of medical institutes. They did succeed in inhibiting the extension of most forms of contract practice to women and children, but only at the cost of encouraging the development of medical institutes which provided for the whole family.

Trying Out New Ideas

Before the 1911 Act several other schemes for the provision of medical care had been tried out by the friendly societies. In Leicester, for instance, since the 1870s the societies had separated medical attendance from dispensing. They had initially tried to organise dispensing through local chemists but had replaced that arrangement with their own dispensary. It supplied not only medicines, but also cod liver oil, dressings and nutritional items not normally supplied by doctors. By 1911 the Leicester societies also had a board of thirty-two doctors who would attend and prescribe for all members. Members could choose freely among them.[57]

Over the years there had been experimentation with panel systems, some based on capitation fees and some not. In 1910 a scheme was under way to extend choice among doctors in the North London District of Manchester Unity. This permitted transfer by right to any lodge doctor in the area who had agreed to enter the scheme. Some 80 per cent of lodge surgeons had agreed to participate.[58]

In 1908 and 1909 the National Federation of Dividing Societies was organising improved medical care for their members who lived at an inconvenient distance from their own society's doctor. Members could pay 1s 1d per quarter by post and secure attendance from any one of a hundred doctors on an approved list. Families would be attended for a further 1s 1d.[59]

Some friendly societies developed 'ticket' systems. In Hampshire in the 1860s, for instance, members of one scheme paid 4s per year. Each member had a supply of tickets which he gave to the doctor at each visit. Doctors then claimed the cash value of the tickets: a home visit was worth 2s, a surgery consultation cost 1s 6d, and medicine without consultation cost a 9d ticket. There were additional payments for accidents and operations.[60] Deposit friendly societies commonly used a ticket system, dividing the cost between the common fund and the member's own account.[61]

In some localities societies experimented with a 'medical pool'.

Members of one society in Hertfordshire paid contributions to the lodge, and two doctors saw them as private patients at ordinary fees. The fees were paid by the lodge from the common fund. In the first year (1882) the scheme cost £32 with 160 members; in 1883, £37 with 161 members; in 1884, £59 with 166 members; and in 1885, £82 with 172 members. The scheme had to be abandoned as too costly and contract practice was reinstated.[62] Such schemes were attempted frequently but were often abandoned, chiefly because they tended to be too expensive.

The National Deposit Friendly Society (NDFS) evolved a unique system, which was much disliked by the BMA. Members paid flat-rate annual contributions which entitled them to claim from the society a fixed proportion (usually two thirds or three quarters) of doctors' fees. The fee paid by the society was 2s 6d for a home visit, inclusive of medicines and 1s 6d per surgery consultation.[63] In 1904 the BMA's medico-political committee investigated the scheme and recommended that no such system should be allowed to develop. They disliked it because doctors serving National Deposit members tended to become an approved panel of practitioners, thus making it difficult for the BMA to achieve its aim of extracting the highest fee affordable by each income group. In each district the NDFS was said to 'distinguish between those medical practitioners who have indicated willingness to accept the scale of charges and those who do not'. And representatives of the society often called on doctors to encourage them to accept work on the society's terms. As a result, said the BMA, society members tended to employ approved practitioners 'to the exclusion of their neighbours, and thus underselling is brought about'.[64] Moreover, doctors often accepted the society's part-payment in full settlement of the account.

The Availability of Contract Practice

Beveridge estimated that the societies had over 4.7 million registered members eligible for sick pay, as already noted. That figure excludes death and burial societies not paying sick pay, yet some such societies did employ doctors on contract terms. A burial club at Macclesfield was one such case.[65] The figure also excludes those in specialised friendly societies, which again did not offer sick pay. But among these were the medical institutes which did employ doctors. Membership was 329,450 in 1910.[66] Most were members of friendly societies and will therefore already have been counted, but some were not. In addition to Beveridge's 4.7 million there were unregistered societies which included those in works clubs. In 1911 there were just over a million miners with their own works clubs. Membership comprised not only miners but also steelworkers and employees of other factories operating in colliery areas. I have argued earlier that at least nine million of the 12 million covered by national insurance were already members of voluntary sick pay schemes. A similar proportion was also eligible for medical care.

Conclusion

The freedom to experiment during the period before the 1911 National Insurance Act allowed consumers to protect themselves from the demands of organised medicine and to encourage higher standards of care. First, liberty enabled medical consumers to organise themselves against the efforts of the medical profession to force up pay and free doctors from accountability to patients for the standard of care. Second, the absence of a public sector monopoly before 1911 enabled different methods of paying for medical care to be attempted and threw up valuable lessons from which others could learn and on which future progress could be based. The 1911 Act led to the dismantling of these arrangements by the state at the behest of the doctors, as Chapter 9 describes.

8

The Classical-Liberal Heyday: 1834-1911

During the nineteenth and twentieth centuries the attitude of the state towards the friendly societies altered radically, providing examples of how the power of the state can be a force for both good and evil, and thereby helping us to get closer to an understanding of the principles which should guide a society devoted to liberty under law. There were three main periods: before 1834 the societies were subject to paternalistic supervision by the justices of the peace; between the 1834 Friendly Societies Act and the 1911 National Insurance Act, liberalism was the general rule; and from 1911 paternalism made its return leading eventually to the near-destruction of the friendly societies in 1948.

Pre-1834 Paternalism

Until the 1830s the attitude of the governing classes towards the friendly societies was dictated partly by their concern to reduce the poor rate by promoting friendly societies and (especially after the French Revolution and during the Napoleonic Wars) partly by a countervailing fear that the societies threatened social order.

The societies were affected by the Seditious Meetings Acts of 1795 and 1817, the Unlawful Societies Act of 1799 and the Combination Acts of 1799-1800. Indeed, the cloud of illegality hung over the affiliated friendly societies until 1846. It was in 1834 that the Tolpuddle Martyrs were sentenced to seven years transportation for establishing the Friendly Society of Agricultural Labourers. Their society was partly a trade union, concerned to maintain the wages of agricultural labourers, and partly a friendly society, concerned to build up a fund on which members and their families could call in times of sickness, accident or other hardship.

The aim of the judge who pronounced sentence had been to suppress the growth of trade unions by making an example of the men of Tolpuddle. He imposed on them the most severe penalty the law allowed. But the Martyrs had not been found guilty of establishing a trade union—which anyway was not illegal—but of administering an unlawful oath. The oath they took differed little from the oaths commonly sworn by the trade unions, friendly societies and Freemasons' lodges of the day. It was an oath of loyalty to other society members and a promise not to disclose society affairs to outsiders. It formed part of an initiation ceremony which included saying a prayer, singing hymns and an exposition of the aims of the society. The six men were far from being criminals. Indeed, their twenty-third rule expressly forbade violence and law-breaking: 'The object of this society can never be promoted by any act or acts of violence, but, on the contrary, all such proceedings must tend to hinder the cause and destroy the society itself. This Order will not countenance any violation of the laws.'

In 1836 after a great public outcry, the Tolpuddle Martyrs were granted a free pardon.[1] Their pardoning reflected the change of mood which was noticeable from the early 1830s onwards and which had led to the return of a Whig Government under Lord Grey in 1831. His administration promptly enacted the Reform Act of 1832 to widen the franchise, and the Poor Law Amendment Act of 1834, which abolished outdoor relief. Edwin Chadwick, summed up the new mood of hostility to paternalism and confidence in human ingenuity. He described how the upper classes had sought to help the poor through charities and profuse expenditure financed from the rates which, he thought, had proved 'the most potent means of retarding the improvement of the labouring population'. The best way for the wealthy to help the poor would be 'in acting *with* the labouring classes rather than *for* them' by enabling them to act for themselves through organisations such as provident institutions.[2]

Liberalism 1834-1911

In 1834, a new Friendly Societies Act was passed embodying the new attitude to friendly societies. They were no longer required to be under the control of the local justices. Instead a light, centralised system of registration was introduced. Before 1834, JPs had been required to satisfy themselves that new societies were desirable and that there was not already another society fulfilling the same need. The 1834 Act removed this restriction altogether. Prior to 1834 JPs had also to be satisfied that the rules of a society were 'fit and proper', but after the Act the government barrister (later the Registrar) had only to be satisfied that rules were 'in conformity with law'. JPs were formerly empowered to establish that the tables of contributions and benefits had been approved by two actuaries or persons skilled in calculation. This requirement was abolished and the aims of friendly societies were widened to include any purpose which was not otherwise illegal.

The evolution of the friendly societies owes much to this liberal framework of law introduced from the 1830s which allowed people to band together to meet their own needs as they believed best. In 1846 the title of Registrar of Friendly Societies was given to the government barrister who had previously registered rules. The first Registrar was John Tidd Pratt, who held office until his death in 1870. He had been responsible for registering the societies since the 1834 Act and was a tireless campaigner for financial soundness within the societies.

The 1846 Friendly Societies Act declared that the Corresponding Societies Act and the Seditious Meetings Act did not apply to friendly societies, but it was not until an Act of 1850 that branches of the affiliated orders were allowed to register and thus protect their funds at law. The 1850 Friendly Societies Act also distinguished between certified and registered societies. Certified societies were those whose tables were approved by the actuary of the National Debt Commissioners; registered societies had only to submit their rules to the Registrar. This distinction, however, was abolished in 1855, though actuarial certification was required if a society offered 'a certain annuity or a certain superannuation'.

Even after 1855 the benefits of registration were few and by far the most valued benefit was recognition under the law, the lack of which had cost the Manchester Unity dear in 1848 when a senior official had absconded with substantial funds. The case came to court but the judge refused to allow Manchester Unity any redress because it was not a legally recognised entity. The importance to the societies of legal recognition can be gauged by comparing Scotland and England. In Scotland the common law and the presence of a public prosecutor gave better protection to unregistered societies, and 84 per cent of Scottish societies did not register. In England, where the common law gave less protection, about one-third of societies were thought to be unregistered after the 1850 Act.[3]

Tidd Pratt's death in 1870 was followed by a Royal Commission which sat from 1870 to 1874 and led to the 1875 Friendly Societies Act which was intended by its sponsors to help make the societies more reliable as insurers. Registered societies were required to have their accounts audited annually, to forward annual returns of receipts and expenditure, quinquennial returns of sickness and mortality, and quinquennial valuations of assets and liabilities. Previously they had not been allowed to invest in land, but after 1875 this limitation was abolished. In addition, dividing societies were allowed to register. From 1875 a new Chief Registrar was appointed, J.M. Ludlow, who retained office until 1891.

Since 1819 the societies had been allowed to invest their funds on advantageous terms with the Commissioners of the National Debt and from 1829 the rate of interest was set at three per cent. Under the 1875 Act, the societies continued to be exempt from certain stamp duties but the rate of interest available from the Commissioners was reduced to two per cent. These attractions were never enough to induce a great many societies to register and the Royal Commission estimated that about half of societies were unregistered in the early 1870s.

Financial Reliability

The nineteenth century saw steady progress in understanding the level of weekly contributions that would enable the promised benefits to be paid, but it took several decades for reliable actuarial tables to become available. The greatest danger for individual members of local clubs was that a society might last a few years and then collapse leaving the older members without support.

Benefits and contributions varied from place to place depending on local circumstances and competition. As new societies were founded, mistakes were sometimes made, throwing up valuable lessons from which others could learn. For instance, sometimes new societies sought to establish themselves by offering lower contributions for the same benefits, or perhaps better benefits. But there was no guarantee that the contributions would be sufficient. Often clubs were formed by men of roughly the same age, but as they grew older they found that they could not recruit younger members. It was also the pattern until well into the nineteenth century to charge uniform contributions, and it was only later as experience grew that contributions graduated according to age became more common. The amount devoted to management expenses also varied. In 1870 an investigator for the Royal Commission found that many of the 230 societies in

Oldham spent part of their funds on conviviality. He claimed this was why most had found it necessary occasionally to suspend benefits, or 'close the box'.[4]

There are two possible approaches to the risk of members' contributions being insufficient to pay benefits. The first is to assume that correct contributions can be scientifically calculated and for the regulator to impose the 'correct' tables on the societies. The other is for each society to be allowed to back its own judgement at its own risk in order that each society can learn from the success or failure of many others.

Legislators veered from one extreme to the other during the nineteenth century. Before 1834 they were inclined to paternalism, and societies were required to have their tables certified by two actuaries. Tables of contributions used at the time, however, proved unreliable. The first attempt to devise such tables had been made by Dr Price in 1789. He estimated that, in societies made up of people under the age of 32, one in forty-eight would be sick. The rate of sickness increased in steps until for 58-64 year olds the rate was estimated to be double. Experience, however, proved his estimate to have been too low.

Between 1834 and the Act of 1850, societies were not required to have their tables approved by an actuary at all, but were under an obligation to submit returns of their sickness and mortality experience every five years. In 1850 paternalism made a temporary comeback. Legislation enabled the societies or branches to register and thus protect their funds at law. The same Act also drew a distinction between certified and registered societies. However, the folly of appointing a single judge of financial soundness had become apparent by 1855.

The first reliable tables had become available in 1845 based on data F.G.P. Neison obtained from the returns made under the 1834 Act, and covering the period 1836-40. Then, in 1850 Henry Ratcliffe, the corresponding secretary of the Manchester Unity, published further reliable tables based on his own society's experience during 1846, 1847 and 1848. He produced further reports in 1862 and 1872.

Did the reliability of Neison's tables of 1845 and Ratcliffe's of 1850 make it 'game, set and match' for the paternalists? In fact, the matter was then confused by the government figures published in 1853 and 1854 by J. Finlaison, the Actuary of the National Debt Office. He was the official charged with certifying financial soundness under the 1850

Act and sewed confusion by adopting a narrow definition of sickness. Instead of basing his estimates of sickness on the actual claims experience of the societies, he defined sickness very narrowly as 'sickness incapacitating from labour, and requiring constant medical treatment, and of limited duration, as contradistinguished from chronic ailment and increpitude'.[5] But the societies were paying out for chronic conditions and members expected them to do so. Tidd Pratt made matters worse by recommending Finlaison's tables and publishing extracts in his first annual report. The Royal Commission commented in 1874, 'There is no doubt that the plan on which these tables were formed has proved unfortunate, and that many societies and even actuaries have made use of the tables without discovering that they were inapplicable to societies which do not limit the benefit to sickness as defined by Mr Finlaison.'[6]

If the state had enforced Finlaison's tables, great harm would have been done. Fortunately in 1855 the distinction between certification and regulation was abolished and the societies allowed to compete. From that year the law remained largely unchanged until 1875. Moreover, after the 1875 Act the legal framework remained essentially liberal, allowing wide latitude for different approaches which yielded a rich harvest of diverse alternatives.

The Struggle Within Manchester Unity

As the first society to become a national organisation, Manchester Unity was also the first to encounter the problems of an aging membership. By the middle of the century it was obvious to Manchester Unity's leaders that insufficient contributions had been paid by members to meet liabilities in old age. In 1845 the usual benefit was 10s sick pay, £10 on the death of a member and from £6-10 on the death of his wife. Contributions were usually 4d, 5d or 6d per week. In 1843 225 Manchester Unity lodges had closed for 'want of funds' and many more had applied for help from the unity. In 1844 Manchester Unity tried to obtain returns from its branches to establish their financial status. Many refused and between the 1844 and 1845 annual meetings lodges with 16,000 members were suspended for failing to submit returns of sickness and their accounts.

From 1845 every lodge was ordered to keep a separate fund for all expenses except sickness and funeral benefit. This was to prevent the annual feast or other convivial activities being financed from the sick and funeral fund. Lodges could still set their own contributions, but within guidelines: 1s (5p) sick pay per week and £1 at death in return for each ½d of contribution per week. The proposals did not guarantee financial viability but established the power of the annual conference to intervene when lodges were in danger of failing. Some lodges seceded but most accepted the new situation.[7]

In fact the 1845 rates were inadequate. According to Neison's tables, the contributions should have been 39s 5d per year, but the actual rate was 22s 9d, 42 per cent too low.[8] Occasionally the societies were described as insolvent, but while he was assistant registrar, Sir Edward Brabrook (later to become Registrar) warned against hasty judgements. The word 'insolvency', he said, was quite out of place.[9] The lodges tended to rely on the recruitment of younger members to cover losses, and it must be remembered, he insisted, that they were not pure insurance societies, they were also fraternities, and so from time to time additional levies were approved by meetings to cover any shortfall. Collections were also taken, and money raised from other sources. Honourary members contributions were sometimes used to subsidise the sick fund, and the unity or the district sometimes baled out lodges in trouble. So it cannot be assumed that the refusal of a lodge to comply with an actuary's wishes was the result of sheer bloody mindedness or of ignorance. Some branches preferred the system of fraternalism to operating on pure insurance lines.

Gradually, however, opinions were changing and within three years of the publication of Manchester Unity's 1850 tables, the Manchester Unity's annual meeting adopted for the first time a graduated scale of contributions based on age at entry. Not all lodges accepted the new rates, but gradually the new system spread.[10]

The 1875 Act: Reliance on Disclosure not Paternalism

Some witnesses who presented evidence to the Royal Commission of 1874 called for the imposition of a centralised social insurance scheme. One proposal was supported by both archbishops, six bishops, 17 lawyers, 35 MPs, 37 chairmen of boards of guardians, 52 JPs, 90 clergymen, plus many others amounting to about 500 men in all, 'besides four ladies', as the report remarks.[11] They called for a government scheme of insurance for sickness, death and old age to be administered through post offices. Fortunately the Commission understood the value of voluntarism and recommended against the proposal, especially because sick pay was so vulnerable to fraud. It took the view that the friendly societies should be improved through compulsory disclosure.

The difficulty for the individual contemplating which friendly society to join was that a somewhat remote benefit was promised in return for current contributions. There was no way of being certain that the contributions would be sufficient. To increase the information at the disposal of potential members, the Act required societies to submit annual and quinquennial accounts and reports and to make quinquennial valuations of assets and liabilities. Failure to comply became a punishable offence.

The chairman of the Royal Commission had been Sir Stafford Northcote, who became Chancellor of the Exchequer in 1874 and steered the new legislation through Parliament. He had two classical-liberal aims: (1) to provide information which would be useful to the societies in framing proper rules and setting contributions and benefits, and (2) to provide information to members of the public to enable them to judge for themselves the position of each society. But he intended to leave the actual management of the societies to the members and their officers.

Under this framework of law no one could inadvertently stumble into membership of a society which would be likely to collapse at the crucial time. However, this did not mean that the local unitary societies disappeared, nor that the dividing societies became extinct. They continued to flourish for the reasons that Beveridge explained in *Voluntary Action*. In particular, it was because they were not mere insurance companies: some were fraternities as well as social clubs, while others provided individuals and their families with a method of saving either for a rainy day or to make a major purchase.

The legal framework of 1875 also allowed new types of organisation to develop as popular requirements altered. No less important, it remained possible for alternative approaches to valuation to evolve. For instance, in 1886 Neison published an analysis of the Foresters distinguishing between the experience of rural and urban areas. As a result, the annual meeting of the Foresters decided to abandon tables based on national experience and resolved that each branch should charge rates based on local data. If a single national scheme had been imposed by the state it would have made it more difficult, if not impossible, to make such beneficial adjustments.

The 1875 Act also formally recognised the affiliated orders as 'registrable units', whereas under the 1855 Act branches were registered separately and could alter their rules or end their connection with the order at will. Earlier legislation had strengthened the independence of the branches from the centre, but the Acts of 1875 and 1876 strengthened the centre. The criterion for registration was the payment of regular contributions to a central fund. Consequently, from 1875 the Manchester Unity and the Foresters, and some smaller orders, arranged for a ½d or 1d contribution per member per annum to a fund for distressed branches.[12] Before 1875 branches had made no contribution, and the head office had been financed by the sale of regalia to branches.

There had always been those who wanted the state to exercise greater control, but their blandishments were resisted until 1911. Previously the state had largely allowed the friendly societies to evolve as they believed best, and voluntary effort had provided a wide variety of medical services and means of providing for income during illness. Chapter 9 tells how the freedom of the societies to evolve was curtailed by the 1911 National Insurance Act, a measure which signalled the end of the liberal approach which had dominated public policy since 1834.

9

1911: National Insurance and the Crowding Out of Mutual Aid

The friendly societies were so successful that their arrangements for social insurance and primary medical care formed the model for the early welfare state.[1] But this, ironically, was their undoing. The 1911 National Insurance Act was originally seen by Lloyd George, who charted it through Parliament, as a way of extending the benefits of friendly society membership to the whole working population. But on its way through the House of Commons the original Bill was radically transformed by powerful vested interests hostile to working-class mutual aid. The organised medical profession had long resented the dominance of the medical consumer, and particularly disliked working-class control of medical 'gentlemen'. The BMA was equally anxious to obtain more pay and higher status for doctors. No less important were the commercial insurance companies, which had long disliked the competition of the non-profit friendly societies and saw the 1911 National Insurance Bill as a threat to their business. They were organised in a powerful trade association, called the 'Combine'.

The BMA and the Combine formed a temporary alliance to extract concessions from the Government at the expense of the friendly societies. The essence of working-class social insurance was democratic self-organization, but amendments to the Bill obtained by the BMA and the Combine undermined it. Doctors' pay had been kept within limits that ordinary manual workers could afford, but under pressure, the Government nearly doubled doctors' incomes and financed this transfer of wealth from insured workers to the medical profession by means of regressive flat-rate national insurance contributions.

Compulsory National Insurance: The Immediate Impact

The government proposal for national insurance, first published in 1910, brought about a change in the attitude of the medical profession. In 1903 contract practice had been described by the *British*

Medical Journal as economically sound in theory and 'in some forms
... one of the pleasantest ways in which a medical man can earn his
living'.[2] But once public discussion of the proposals began, feelings
changed. As one doctor put it, with compulsory state insurance the
raison d'être of contract practice had gone:

> We now resume our place as medical practitioners pure and simple,
> ready as sellers to give our services to the buyer, who is now not the
> poverty-stricken wage earner, but the solvent State Insurance Company.[3]

Doctors have often been seen as arch-enemies of state intervention, an impression reinforced by their vigorous initial opposition to
the government plan. But the disagreement was about the terms;
doctors had no objection to a state takeover as a matter of principle
so long as it increased their pay, status and control.[4]

The Combine

By 1910 the commercial insurance industry had become too powerful
for the Government to ignore. At the end of that year 28.5 million
funeral benefit policies were in force with a total face value of over
£285 million. Each year a further 10 million policies were being sold.
Ninety per cent of this business was controlled by 12 large companies,
and the industry was well organised through its association, known
as the 'Combine'. About 100,000 men were employed in the industry,
of whom around 70,000 were full-time door-to-door salesmen. They
derived their income from a commission on each policy sold, varying
between 20 and 30 per cent of the premium. The total premium due
to an agent in a week was called the 'book'. Books were bought and
sold and therefore represented a considerable investment on the part
of collectors.

Before William Braithwaite, assistant secretary at the Board of
Inland Revenue, had prepared the detailed scheme, the insurance
companies had extracted a major concession from Lloyd George, the
Chancellor of the Exchequer. Initially, he had intended the legislation
to provide for a widows' and orphans' benefit but the insurance
companies successfully opposed the proposal because they feared it
would make their death benefit policies less attractive.

The industry was powerful, not so much because of its wealth but
because of the disciplined army of 70,000 collectors at its disposal.
Their influence over opinion was much feared by the Liberal Government, not least because its majority in Parliament had been reduced

in January 1910, obliging it to rely for survival on the support of the Labour party. Lloyd George was reluctant to drop the widows' and orphans' pension from the scheme but eventually did so for fear of the insurance companies:

> however desirable it may be to substitute state insurance ... any Party that attempted it would instantly incur the relentless hostility of all these agents and collectors. They visit every house, they are indefatigable, they are often very intelligent, and a government which attempted to take over their work without first securing the cooperation of the other Party would inevitably fail in its undertaking; so that, if a scheme of national insurance is taken in hand by any Party Government, it must be confined to invalidity, and the most urgent and pitiable cases of all must be left out.[5]

As the bill passed through Parliament it was further transformed. The first draft of the Bill, published in May 1911, permitted the friendly societies to become 'approved societies' and excluded the insurance companies altogether. Two of the Bill's provisions, both deliberately inserted by Braithwaite, prevented insurance companies from becoming approved societies. The first, Clause 21(2)(3)(4), required each approved society to establish local management committees of members unless they already had branches. The second was Clause 18(2), subsection (ii) of which required that an approved society 'must be precluded by its constitution from distributing any of its funds otherwise than by way of benefits (whether benefits under this Act or not) amongst its members'. Subsection (iii) required that 'its affairs must be subject to the absolute control of its members', and subsection (iv) that 'its constitution must provide for the election of all its committees, representatives, and officers by its members'.[6]

The Combine set out to have these provisions removed. Their army of agents was encouraged to engage in vigorous lobbying, a task they undertook with enthusiasm, and by the end of June 1911 an important concession had already been won. Clause 18(2)(ii), which would have made the distribution of profits to shareholders unlawful, was deleted.

At about the same time the Combine gained a valuable ally, the British Medical Association. Together, the Combine and the BMA obtained two other crucial concessions. The requirement that approved societies should have local management committees was withdrawn; and medical benefit was to be administered, not by approved societies, but by local health committees (later called insurance committees).

The friendly societies were slow to react to these changes, but in September and October they began to fight the influence of the Combine. They sought the re-instatement of the requirement that approved societies be non-profit making and self-governing. Not only were their efforts in vain, but they went on to suffer a third defeat. Subsections (iii) and (iv) of Clause 18(2) made it impossible for insurance companies to continue operating on centralised business lines and the Combine sought their removal from the Bill. Not yet defeated, the friendly societies pressed for their retention. But, after a long campaign, Clause 18(2) was redrafted to suit the Combine. Braithwaite commented on this amendment:

> from this moment, at the bottom of my heart, I lost a great deal of my interest in the Bill. I regard the whole transaction as a betrayal of the spirit of the Bill, for whilst these Collecting Societies [the Combine] were entitled to come in, they should have done so under control and not as controllers.[7]

If the amendments to the Bill had been intended to extend competition to the advantage of consumers, they might not have been wholly without merit. But in reality the amendments played into the hands of organised medicine by eliminating the chief means by which consumers were able to defend themselves against bad service and high fees.

Consumer Control After 1911

The friendly societies had for many decades encouraged doctors to improve the standard of their services through competition. In addition, the friendly societies also evolved complaints procedures to keep doctors on their toes.

The government also provided complaints machinery under the 1911 Act, but it was much inferior. As Professor Rudolf Klein has argued, the 1911 Act 'marked a giant step forward in the emancipation of the medical profession from lay control'. The complaints machinery of 1911 was introduced 'not as an attempt to fortify the position of the consumer but as a salvage operation designed to save something from the wreck of lay control over medical services'. The 1911 deal represents 'the first rung in the ladder leading to the syndicalist system of professional control over the health services'.[8]

The friendly society tradition was based on the rules of natural justice. There are two main principles: *audi alteram partem*, 'hear the other side'; and *nemo judex in causa sua*, 'no man may be a judge in his own cause'. Underlying this philosophy was the belief that both sides had an equal right to have their case heard and that essential to the, process was the independence of those judging the issue. Friendly society rules therefore provided for the appointment of arbitration committees comprised of individuals with no axe to grind.

The view of the doctors was the opposite: no one should judge professional conduct except the professional. Doctors have often asserted that this notion is in the public interest, but without exception it has been accompanied by an ethic of professional loyalty which strongly frowned upon criticism of one's fellows.

Arrangements for the Uninsured in the 1930s

The period from 1913 to 1948 is of particular interest because it makes possible a comparison between market provision and state provision. The working population was covered by the national insurance scheme, but wives and children were not. They obtained health care in the marketplace.

The main types of provision were: the outpatient departments of the voluntary hospitals, the free dispensaries, the provident dispensaries, friendly society lodge practice, insurance against medical fees (including friendly society approved panels), public medical services, private doctor's clubs, works clubs, and friendly society medical institutes.

Many people continued to use outpatient departments instead of a GP, even though by the 1930s many voluntary hospitals were encouraging or even requiring patients to go to their GP first. In 1935 there were 1,103 voluntary hospitals, which admitted 1.2 million inpatients and attended 5.6 million outpatients.[9] Some public hospitals also performed a similar role.

Free dispensaries financed by charities continued to function in many large towns. In the mid 1930s there were over twenty in the London area alone. Provident dispensaries also continued to operate. In the London area there were nearly twenty. The Battersea Provident Dispensary was one of the largest with over 6,000 members in 1936. Single persons paid 3d a week, doctors on its panel received a capitation fee of 6s.[10]

A number of private medical clubs continued to function, but it is impossible to estimate how many persons were covered. In the judgement of the BMA survey of 1938-39 private clubs were 'gradually dying out'. In the 'great majority' of cases divisional secretaries reported that there were no private clubs, often because they had been absorbed into public medical services. Rates tended to be a least 3d a week, although local conventions varied enormously.[11] By the late 1930s, it is unlikely that more than 100,000 persons were covered by private club membership.

Many factories and all collieries provided medical attendance. Some were managed by the employer and some by committees representing employees. Usually such schemes covered families as well as employees. Political and Economic Planning (PEP), carried out a major study but felt unable to estimate the number covered. However, we know that there were still about one million miners in the mid 1930s. Their dependants must have accounted for between two and two-and-a-half million people.

The BMA had been promoting the establishment of 'public medical services'. The largest was in London, and by 1937 throughout the country there were nearly eighty services with 650,000 subscribers. A survey of fifty-one public medical services found that for each subscription 1.86 persons were 'at risk'. On this basis a total of about 1.2 million people were covered by public medical services. About 4,000 doctors were involved, receiving capitation fees averaging 11s 2d, with large towns more expensive than rural areas.[12] Expansion in the 1930s had been rapid. In 1932 there had been only thirty-two public medical services.

Friendly Society Lodge Practice

Most of those who had been covered by lodge practice before 1911 were covered by national insurance, but the lodges continued to provide for the women and children who were outside the national insurance scheme. According to the BMA's surveys of contract practice rates carried out in 1935-36 and 1938-39, contract practice to adult members of friendly societies was 'steadily diminishing'. But it was still to be found in many areas. Rates varied a good deal, depending on competition. In 1935-36, the annual fee in Bath was 5s; in Birmingham, 11s; in Chesterfield, 13s; Norwich, 12s; Kent 6s; and in Barnsley, 10s. The highest was 16s, in Ely.[13]

The BMA surveys of 1935-36 and 1938-39 were incomplete, but the BMA believed that 90 per cent of existing contract schemes had been covered. The surveys were concerned with rates of pay and not the number insured, but some indications are provided. Combining the BMA's findings with the figures published by the Registrar of Friendly Societies, allows us to estimate the number of people obtaining medical care through the friendly societies.

In 1930 there were 700 juvenile friendly societies with 185,000 members. Friendly societies with branches had 2,982,000 members; dividing societies 499,000; and friendly societies without branches paying sick benefit on accumulating principles had 1,152,000 members. Not all these members were insured for medical care, and many were covered by national insurance but had opted to take out additional voluntary sickness or other insurance.

The 185,000 members of the juvenile societies would have been covered for medical care. In addition, the adult friendly societies had junior members. The friendly societies with branches had 134,000 members aged under sixteen in 1930; the sickness benefit societies (on accumulating principles) had 122,000; and the dividing societies, 5,000; a total of 446,000 juvenile members. The societies with branches had 2,189,000 members aged over sixteen; the accumulating societies 947,000; and the dividing societies 370,000. Of the total adult membership of 3,506,000 the great majority of women members would have subscribed for medical care. The Registrar did not publish separate figures for male and female members, but the evidence of the National Conference of Friendly Societies to the Beveridge committee of 1942 suggests that females comprised about a quarter of total voluntary membership. In 1941, 24 per cent of the 4.6 million members were female.[14] On this formula, of the 3.5 million adult voluntary members in 1930 around 840,000 would have been women. Most would have paid for medical benefit.[15] Some of the male members would also have attended lodge doctors. If only 10 per cent did so it would suggest a figure of about 280,000. All told, at least somewhere in the region of 1.5 million persons including children who were members of the adult friendly societies as well as special juvenile societies, must have been obtaining medical care through friendly societies other than deposit societies in the mid 1930s. This estimate is based on registered friendly society membership and takes no account of unregistered friendly societies.

Insurance Against Medical Fees

After the 1911 Act some friendly societies developed new schemes for insurance against doctors' fees. Some medical schemes provided for repayment of the whole fee, and some for part. In a few cases any doctor could be consulted and a repayment of whatever fee he charged could be claimed. In most cases a doctor had to be selected from a panel of doctors who had agreed to charge specified fees.

On the introduction of national insurance in 1911, the South London District of the Manchester Unity established a fee-for-service scheme. Members initially contributed 1d a week (soon increased to 2d) into a common fund, the district medical aid fund. Members could consult any doctor, pay the bill and recover the amount paid from the fund. Doctors charged 3s per home visit and 2s for a surgery consultation. By 1925 there were 6,000 subscribers to the financially successful scheme. Over the twelve years, average annual expenditure had been about £2,000.[16] Such 'medical pools' as they were often called, were also successful in some other areas, such as Swadlincote, Coalville, and Wolverton, but their success had only been accomplished by placing a limit on the amounts doctors were permitted to charge.[17]

Schemes run on part-payment principles (co-insurance) expanded rapidly. In 1936, over 1.3 million members of the National Deposit Friendly Society were covered for payment of a proportion of doctors' bills, as were 57,000 members of the Teachers Provident Society.[18] Until 1948, National Deposit Friendly Society members paid 2s 6d for a surgery attendance and 3s 6d for a home visit, including medicine. The society reimbursed either two-thirds or three-quarters of the fee (above p. 86).[19] However, according to the BMA, a 'considerable number' of doctors continued to accept the National Deposit payment alone in full settlement of the account, despite long-standing BMA criticism of the practice.[20]

How Many Were Covered?

In 1939 Great Britain had a population of 46.5 million. Of these, about 19 million were covered by national insurance. Outpatient departments of both voluntary and public hospitals must have served about six million; the charitable and provident dispensaries perhaps 300,000; the lodges 1.5 million; the medical institutes 150,000; fee-for-service insurance two million; public medical services 1.2 million; private doctors' clubs 100,000; and works clubs (including medical aid societies) about three million. On these estimates about 14.2 million individuals would have been covered by the above schemes. It seems probable that at least another million would have been covered by unregistered friendly societies. The remaining 12 million or so would have paid private fees.

Competition

Most notable among the organisations which offered competition and restrained medical fees were the friendly society medical institutes and the Welsh medical aid societies. In the 1930s the medical institutes had only about 150,000 voluntary members (in addition to national insurance members), but they were distributed throughout England in over 60 large towns. Only one serious competitor in a locality was required to upset BMA price-fixing, and the medical institutes consequently had an effect on prices out of all proportion to the size of their membership. This market power earned them the implacable hostility of the medical profession and, as a result, when the NHS was being planned the BMA's hostility was decisive in ensuring that no role at all was permitted for medical institutes.

Throughout the life of the panel system, the BMA kept the Ministry of Health under constant pressure to discriminate against the medical institutes and medical aid societies. In March 1921, for instance, Alfred Cox wrote to the Ministry on behalf of the BMA complaining that the Norwich Friendly Societies Medical Institute was charging 3s a quarter for juvenile members. The BMA felt this was too low and accused the institute of subsidising juveniles out of their income from the national insurance scheme. Cox wrote again on 22 April emphasising that the BMA 'strongly objects' to the subsidisation of the non-insured. The Permanent Secretary (R.W. Harris) replied that he could not continue the correspondence on an official footing but proposed a private chat when Cox was next in the Ministry. On 7 May Cox called in for his chat. An official note records the BMA's reasoning:

> From the BMA point of view it is particularly important that the assumption that these uninsured juveniles can be treated for the same charge as an insured person should not be established as a precedent which might be used in the event of the extension of GP treatment to the general population.[21]

106

The best available evidence is contained in the BMA surveys of 1935-36 and 1938-39. These show that many rates were below national insurance capitation fees. Medical institutes, in particular, kept rates down. The Reading public medical service (run by the BMA) had the lowest fees in the whole country and they were told that this was causing the BMA's public medical services sub-committee 'considerable anxiety'. The Reading doctors told the BMA that it was impossible to raise charges because of active competition from the Amalgamated Friendly Societies of Reading.

Works clubs also offered competition. In South Wales, where the medical aid societies were dominant, arrangements were said to have 'improved' (i.e. they had become less competitive) but in other areas, and notably in Yorkshire, fees were 'not satisfactory'. The branch council was demanding 4d a week for men and boys, but going rates were lower. Out of thirteen cases in the survey report, weekly rates in seven were 3d, and in three others 3½d.[22]

To sum up: there were still considerable competitive pressures preventing the BMA from unilaterally fixing rates. Even against the background of national insurance and a professional policy of seeking increases up to government rates in the private contract sector, the profession lacked the power to get its way. This applied not only to contract practice. When patients insured against medical fees the BMA was also unable to prevent doctors accepting, for instance, the two-thirds contribution of the National Deposit Friendly Society in full settlement of accounts. Consumer combinations to offer countervailing power to the organised profession survived twenty years of pressure to obliterate them.

Who Benefited From National Insurance?

The 1911 National Insurance Act weakened the power of the medical consumer, but what effect did it have on medical incomes? The leading complaint voiced by doctors before the 1911 Act was that they were underpaid. As a result of the government scheme, they secured a very large increase in their incomes. But this did not stem the tide of criticism. After 1911, doctors' complaints about low fees—so often taken at face value by critics of pre-1911 health care—were directed at the government instead of the friendly societies. Initially the government had offered the doctors 6s per insured patient, including medicine. This was a generous offer, for the minimum contract practice rate then being demanded by the BMA was 5s, itself higher than some market rates. In February 1912 the BMA demanded 8s 6d, excluding medicine.

A survey of doctors' incomes was carried out by Sir William Plender, who was asked to visit six towns, three selected by the Insurance Commission and three by the BMA. He studied the income of doctors in 1910 and 1911 in Cardiff, Darlington, Darwen, Dundee, Norwich and St Albans. He approached 265 doctors, of whom fifty-one refused access to their records. Forty of the fifty-one were in Cardiff, and for this reason Cardiff was dropped from the study.

Sir William reported in July that in the remaining five towns the average annual gross income of doctors in private practice, less a proportion for bad debts, was 4s 2d per patient. If income from contract patients was added, the average worked out at 4s 1¾d. The average annual capitation fee being paid was 3s 11d. The average of 4s 2d requires adjustment because Dundee doctors did not dispense medicines. In an estimate prepared by the Insurance Commission for England, 4s 5d was suggested as a more accurate figure, allowing for the cost of medicines in Dundee.[23]

The *British Medical Journal* immediately denounced Plender's findings as biased and incorrect, and the BMA continued to press for an increase in the 6s being offered. The government responded by raising its offer to 7s 6d. This was also rejected. On 23 October the government finally raised its offer to 9s (including medicines). This offer was also rejected by the BMA.

By this time, however, rifts were beginning to appear within the medical profession. The leadership of the BMA was out of touch with the rank and file, who knew only too well that acceptance of 9s would mean the near doubling of their incomes. In January 1913 the 9s offer was accepted.[24]

In the years leading up to the 1911 Act the unity sought by many doctors was lacking. But, one of the chief results of national insurance was that it stimulated the medical profession to unite at the expense of the consumer. Doctors organised a campaign to transform the national insurance scheme into one that benefited them at the expense of medical consumers, and particularly friendly society members. As a result of their agitation between 1910 and 1912, the doctors made substantial gains: most notably, they freed themselves from lay control, insinuated themselves into the machinery of the state, and nearly doubled their fees.

10

1948: The Eradication of Mutual Aid

The legislation of 1911 had incorporated the friendly societies into the state national insurance scheme. The virtue of voluntarism is that a variety of methods of provision can develop to meet the differing needs of individuals and families. The affiliated friendly societies provided one approach but they were not everyone's cup of tea and many preferred the different systems of the more centralised societies like the Hearts of Oak or the National Deposit Friendly Society. This very variety, however, became a problem under the state scheme, for voices began to complain that it was unfair that different benefits were received for the same compulsory contribution.

The Beveridge Report of 1942 described what these differences had come to mean by the late 1930s. Under the approved-society system each society was valued at five-yearly intervals and after providing for reserves a surplus or deficiency was calculated. The surplus could be spent on additional benefits for members. The fifth valuation in 1938 allowed societies with 88 per cent of the insured men and 81 per cent of the insured women to pay additional benefits. The surplus was £5,850,000 when total expenditure was about £35m. Of this £5,850,000, £2,200,000 was paid in additional cash benefits and £3,650,000 in benefits in kind, largely dental and ophthalmic care, medical appliances and convalescent homes. Additional sickness and disablement benefits were paid by societies representing 63 per cent of insured men. About £250,000 was spent on maternity benefits.[1]

The Beveridge Report recommended a single contribution and a single benefit agency to administer the scheme. However, Beveridge was keen that friendly societies should be allowed to act as agents for the payment of state benefit and to offer additional services to members purchased with voluntary contributions.[2] To Beveridge's great disappointment his proposal was rejected by the Government.

The result was a monolithic state system for benefits and medical care. The remainder of the chapter is devoted to an example of what this meant in practice for the medical institutes and the medical aid societies of the Welsh miners, which had proved their pioneering worth despite the prolonged antipathy of organised medicine.

It is a detailed case study, but it is worth examination because it reveals the mentality of the period, and in particular it shows how the intellectual leaders of the day failed to understand the value of diversity in allowing room for human progress. Beveridge himself warned in *The Times* before the second reading of the National Insurance Bill in February 1946, that it would be a costly mistake to refuse the friendly societies a continuing role. To set up an 'all-embracing State machine will be final', warned Beveridge, whereas to admit the friendly societies would 'leave room for experiment and trial'.[3] But his words were ignored.

The Demise of the Medical Institutes

Throughout the 1920s and 1930s the medical institutes had exercised a restraining effect on medical fees to the advantage of the consumer. The BMA seized the opportunity offered by the new National Health Service to wipe out the medical institutes for good.

During the Second World War there was much discussion of how primary medical care should be organised. One plan followed another in quick succession including the 'Brown Plan', the White Paper of 1944, and the 'Willink Plan'. When the National Health Service Bill was passed in 1946, the NHS general practitioner service turned out to be very like the old 1911 panel system. The insurance committees were replaced by local executive councils. There was a degree of central control of the GP service through the Medical Practices Committee. Capitation payment was retained, and private practice was to continue, but the sale of practices was forbidden.

The wartime Coalition Government had begun to plan a comprehensive medical service in February 1943, and in March Ernest Brown, Minister of Health, announced his proposals. The South Wales and Monmouthshire Alliance of Medical Aid Societies (SWMA), worried about their future role under the plan, asked to meet the Minister but was rebuffed. In December 1943 Henry Willink became Minister, and two months later published a White Paper, *A National Health Service*, which proposed to 'weld together' existing institutions. In March 1944 the Friendly Societies' Medical Alliance (FSMA) inquired how this 'welding' would be carried out, and subsequently a joint conference of the FSMA and the SWMA decided to ask the Minister why the

White Paper did not refer to 'approved institutions', as the medical institutes were known. The Minister agreed to meet both organisations in April 1944 and subsequently Willink wrote to Sir Geoffrey Shakespeare, the sympathetic MP for Norwich, assuring him that the medical institutes were not being overlooked: 'their valuable pioneering work is fully appreciated'.[4]

The friendly societies sought further meetings with the Minister throughout 1944. Civil servants advised him to decline to meet them until after the BMA's Representative Meeting in December. One senior adviser told Willink he suspected the alliances would merely ask 'that their existence should be preserved in the NHS... rather than submit helpful suggestions on the general form the GP service should take'. There was thus no real point in meeting them.

In December, civil servants finally advised that a meeting with the alliances *should* be held. One of them had scrawled on the back of a letter from the FSMA dated 11 December:

> I do not quite see how these people can be put off any longer. Indeed, I should have thought it was better now than later, since it is easier now to give a non-committal answer on the ground that there are still so many doubtful factors.[5]

'Killing Off' the Competition

A civil service memorandum to the Minister dated 18 January 1945 advised:

> Their case is poor. They have always been disliked by the medical profession; they are not much thought of by the Department; and the Royal Commission of 1926 said they were 'anomalous'.[6]

Moreover, the Minister was told, their past advantage in providing a wider range of services than under the panel system would disappear under the new scheme. The Minister should therefore 'listen to their case and hold out no hopes, without finally announcing any decision to kill them'. In these circumstances it would be better to 'see them soon and get it over'. A personal meeting with the Minister was thought best because of the interest in the matter displayed by Sir Geoffrey Shakespeare. And the minister was advised with the characteristic deviousness of public officials that, because 'if we are in fact in the end going to kill them [they will] not then be able to complain that they have not been able to put their case in the highest quarters.'[7] The alliances finally met the Minister in February 1945.

The medical institutes were never taken seriously by the Government and the Minister received a constant stream of advice from civil servants that they should be abandoned. The advice was invariably misleading and of a very low calibre. It was of the kind that flourishes because it is given in secret and cannot therefore be challenged publicly. The friendly societies were simply seen as 'anomalous'. Above all, civil servants appear to have devoutly believed that the NHS would be a vast improvement on the *status quo*:

> ... the societies cannot command the whole range of services which the patient is to be offered in the new scheme. [If] these services are not all at the societies' command, they cannot keep up with the standard elsewhere even if they are better at the start.[8]

In other words, the medical institutes could not possibly be better than the planned NHS; and even if they were, they soon would not be. The assumption appeared to be that the NHS would improve with time, whereas the institutes would not, despite their well-known long record of constant improvement. On the draft version of the above note to the Minister the contradiction had been spotted: the word 'better' had been ringed in pencil and a question mark placed in the margin. But it remained in the final version.

A proposal that the institutes could become agents for the Ministry of Health was strongly rejected. An agency agreement would mean:

> ... first, increased costs of administration, and secondly, the interposition of an extra link in the chain of responsibility—the doctor is responsible to the Society, which is responsible to the Health Service Authorities or the local 'insurance' committee, which are responsible to the patient's representatives, namely, Parliament. Any such extra link weakens the doctor's responsibilities to the patient and makes, e.g., complaints machinery more difficult to work, as has been found in practice.[9]

It would also prevent 'so free a choice of doctor'. Moreover, the argument ran, the profession (the producer) was hostile to the institutes (the consumer), and to support institutes would therefore be to alienate the profession. It was also felt that to allow any 'contracting out' or other arrangements would set a precedent such that before long groups like 'Christian Scientists and nature healers' would be demanding to be included.

Civil Service Ignorance

The memorandum which had been submitted to the Minister by the FSMA and the SWMA in February 1945 was answered point by point. The institutes observed that, because their medical officers consulted patients in the same premises, close co-operation and consultation were more easy. Apparently oblivious of his Department's espousal of health centres for this very reason, an official responded: 'Agreed, but a centralised service does not suit *all* patients, or all doctors'.

The institutes remarked that medical officers and dispensers could also co-operate more easily. The answer they received was that 'the general principle was that doctors should not dispense; centralised services are not the most convenient in all cases'. The official seemed unaware that medical institutes were not being proposed for all cases, only for those who wanted them.

The institutes further noted that their premises were purpose-built. The answer: 'Yes, but the premises are not always very good'. Premises did indeed vary, but they were among the best available anywhere.

The institutes also reminded the Government that they did not work for a profit. It is difficult to believe that the answer they received on this point was sincere: 'The fact that the Institutions do not work for profit should mean that there is no financial hardship if they are merged in the new service and lose their identity'. The provision of consultative and specialist services by the institutes was said to be 'good as far as it goes but the comprehensive service must go further'.

False Reassurance From The Government

At the February 1945 meeting, Willink disingenuously assured the FSMA and SWMA delegates that the Government's object was not 'to destroy existing institutions but to make the best use of the facilities they offered'.[10] The medical institutes were reassured. Nevertheless, at the General Election of July 1945, they contacted MPs in all areas where there was a medical institute to ask if they supported the preservation of approved institutions. The response was favourable and the FSMA was surprised by the 'almost total unanimity' of the reactions.[11]

The delegation which was received by the Minister in February 1945 had been accompanied by two MPs. One was Aneurin Bevan, who fully supported the SWMA at the meeting. In July he became Minister and began signing the same kinds of letters, drafted by the same officials, that Willink and Brown had signed before him. In September the SWMA asked to meet Bevan. He replied that it was 'too early'; he had not made up his mind how to proceed. In late October he put them off again. The following month the FSMA and the SWMA jointly approached the Minister for a meeting. Bevan declined once again, telling them that the 'general issues' were still under review. It was still too early. Finally, a meeting was agreed for January 1946.

Bevan began that meeting by admitting that he was 'somewhat embarrassed'. He was asked if he would like to see the alliance's statement in support of their case for continued existence but replied:

> I know the valuable services rendered by Associations. I have been closely associated with them for many years, even from boyhood, so I cannot be told more than I already know, and it would therefore be a waste of your time and mine to go over the matter again. I will therefore outline to you the Government's Scheme.[12]

Bevan presented the ten delegates with an outline of the proposal. It was to be based 'primarily on health centres, a field in which the Medical Aid Societies had done valuable pioneering'. In the new health centres doctors were to be 'in consultation with each other'. Medical institute doctors 'would therefore be in isolation'. There was to be a distribution of doctors to areas in which they were most needed. 'How could we do that with your doctors?', Bevan asked. They were told that the scheme 'left no proper place for indirect agencies' like medical institutes. But they were assured that their experience would not be wasted and that there would be 'ample work' on the various committees concerned with administering the new scheme. But, Bevan added, there was no reason why the institutes could not provide benefits additional to the state scheme. A delegate pointed out that there would not be much scope for this in a 'full and comprehensive service'.

Bevan was again reminded of the comprehensive services available in Swindon and Tredegar. Were they now, a delegate asked, 'to be thrown on the scrap heap as redundant?' Bevan replied: 'I very much appreciate the splendid work you have done and are still doing. I am not emotional about Institutions but I am about people'. The Cabinet, he said, were 'determined not to have the scheme cluttered up by other agencies'. His conclusion was that: 'You have shown us the way and by your very efficiency you have brought about your own cessation'.[13]

Naive Faith in Collectivism

Three very closely related, but unspoken, notions seem to have been at the root of the Government's thinking. The first was a simple faith in the superiority of government provision over market provision. Even though developments in the health-care market outside the government scheme were considerable, and often provided a model for reformers intent on forcing everyone into a single government scheme, freedom from government interference continued to be poorly valued. By the 1930s, after some years of government intervention, all improvements were taken by progressive opinion to be the result of the government scheme and all problems the result of the continuing inadequacy of the market-place or the unsatisfactory (but easily remediable) nature of previous government intervention. Early mistakes were not seen as inherent in government intervention as such, but rather as arising from failures of personnel or programme. No satisfactory effort was made to appraise the market as an alternative to intervention. If the market *was* compared, it was the market before intervention—as if no change would have occurred without government interference. Nor was there any recognition that government might inadvertently have stifled some beneficial changes.

Enthusiasts for a state monopoly passionately believed that the new scheme was going to be the best, and therefore to allow any other kind of organisation to continue in being was pointless. It was inconceivable that any alternative would be better.

Closely allied to this simple faith in the superiority of government was a second notion which Hayek has called the 'synoptic delusion'.[14] The notion is that a single person can hold in his mind all the facts relevant to some social problem. The PEP report on Britain's health services provides an example of the synoptic delusion, and of its contradictory character:

> The mere fact that no comprehensive approach to the health services was available and that it has taken a group of ordinarily intelligent people three years to hammer out this preliminary synthesis, is conclusive proof that the subject was in a serious state of confusion. The fact that the elementary information here given had to be collected by prolonged

inquiry from so many different persons and agencies is itself a criticism for those who believe, as we do, that it is important to try to look at these services as a whole, and to judge how they are doing their job by examining them in relation to one another and to the needs they exist to satisfy. No one can be surprised if sectional and one-sided views are prevalent so long as the basis for a balanced and comprehensive view does not exist.[15]

Having made this claim, the report proceeds to complain on the very next line that it is difficult to find a satisfactory answer to the question 'What are the health services?' Its authors were, it seems, demanding a comprehensive view of a subject which they believed to be very complex and the boundaries of which they regarded as indistinct. It is tempting to conclude that one of the reasons they wanted a 'comprehensive system' was simply their frustration as professional researchers with the difficulties of investigating a complex subject. On several occasions the PEP report complains about the difficulty of gathering information about the non-state schemes. For example, referring to works clubs it says: 'Again, owing to the individual and *unorganised* nature of these insurances, it is impossible to ascertain the extent of provision'.[16] 'Unorganised' meant uncentralised, for plainly the schemes were organised in the ordinary sense.

The third notion was that progress was inevitable. All thought was being directed to creating what was intended to be the best health service attainable. That some institutional structures are more amenable to progress than others was not on the agenda in 1945 and 1946. Even though the pioneering work of the medical institutes was freely acknowledged, it appears to have been assumed that there would no longer be any need for pioneering institutions. The state scheme would take care of progress.

A letter to Anthony Eden's private secretary, written by Bevan's private secretary in April 1946 (no doubt with his approval), typifies the thinking of the day: 'We realise the splendid work' of the medical aid associations such as the Leamington Provident Dispensary. The reasons their services will no longer be necessary 'will be simply that provision by public organisation and from public funds will have caught up with pioneer voluntary effort in that sphere'.[17] This viewpoint shows no awareness that a state monopoly is very inferior to the market in facilitating improvement.

The National Health Service Bill was published in March 1946, by which time the SWMA members had resigned themselves to their fate and were beginning to press for assurances that existing staff would be employed by the NHS. The 51 medical institutes in England and Wales employed about 250 staff, around 100 of whom were full time. As an accidental outcome of the crushing of the medical institutes, around a dozen of their employees lost their livelihoods without compensation when the NHS came into being on 5 July 1948.

Fears That The NHS Would Be Inferior

The lay staff of the medical institutes were not the only 'accidental' casualties of the NHS. On 8 June 1948, with only four weeks to go before the NHS officially came into being, the SWMA brought information to Bevan's attention which appears to have alarmed him. It seemed that, in some areas, health-care provision was going to worse after 5 July than before.

On 12 May 1948 an official of the Monmouthshire executive council had told the Welsh Board of Health that the new pharmaceutical service would be unsatisfactory in Tredegar. When the doctors of the Tredegar medical aid society, who carried out the dispensing, stopped doing so on 5 July—as the new scheme required—the two pharmacies in the town 'could not ... provide a service equal to the present'.[18] At the 8 June meeting, Bevan was reminded of this and other problems. He said he did not want the dispensing to go to the pharmacies because 'in four or five years' health centres would be built and the dispensing would then have to go back to the health centres (a very optimistic belief as it turned out). He suggested that the premises of the medical aid societies should be declared 'provisional health centres'.

In a note describing the Minister's feelings after that meeting, Bevan was said to be:

> not at all satisfied that the Local Health Authorities in Monmouthshire and Glamorgan had taken adequate steps to ensure that the health facilities available after the 5 July would be at least as efficient as those available under the Medical Aid Societies.[19]

And Bevan minuted his concerns for the benefit of Ministry staff. He emphasised two points: (i) the service provided after the appointed day must be at least as good as the day before; and (ii) where a medical aid society did not want its services to be taken over by a commercial chemist, it should be allowed to continue as a health centre, even if the building was not suitable. 'Anything could be designated a Health Centre', he insisted, and it could be improved later. On 9 June 1948 an instruction was issued embodying these principles.

Bevan's Feeble Reaction

Bevan's decision was never fully implemented, however. The premises at Tredegar, Ebbw Vale and Blaenavon were considered suitable for use as health centres and the remainder were not. At an angry meeting with the SWMA, officials of the Welsh Board of Health told the delegation that Bevan had originally intended to declare *all* the premises of the medical aid societies provisional health centres, but that he had eventually been prevailed upon by his officials not to do so.

On 1 July 1948, Bevan received a report from the Welsh Board of Health describing exactly what his revised decision would mean. The medical aid societies were carrying out dispensing from 19 centres in South Wales. They had two chemists and four dispensers, and the remaining dispensing was carried out by society doctors. The difficulty at Tredegar was resolved by taking over the premises as a health centre. In other areas doctors would be allowed to continue dispensing. Where commercial chemists were to take over, officials told Bevan that the new service would be satisfactory except in three places: Cwm (Ebbw Vale), Llwynpia (Mid Rhondda) and Pontlottyn. Bevan was warned that his approval of the new arrangements could well mean 'trouble' in the Rhondda, although the position 'might be eased if it could be explained to the local people that a much better pharmaceutical service should result'. At Neath there was a 'small but excellent dispensary', but this would be displaced by a chemist's shop. At mid-Rhondda the dispenser was disabled. He was reported to have provided a good service for many years. Nevertheless he eventually lost his job.[20]

Why did Bevan reverse his promised decision? Officials appear to have feared bad publicity for the NHS. They told the SWMA on 4 July that they 'did *not* want to see press photographers publishing pictures of "provisional" health centres such as would be set up in Glamorgan'.[21] The Government, it seems, was trapped by its own rhetoric. The NHS was 'comprehensive', it was 'the best', and so *nothing*—however true it might be—could be allowed to contradict these claims. The premises of some of the medical aid societies were

118

felt to be too small. Thus it was better to have nothing, and even better to have an inferior service supplied by a commercial chemist, than to let the press claim the NHS was not 'the best'.

The spokesmen for the SWMA were said to be in a 'very angry mood' and officials felt the situation promised to become 'very ugly'. At one stage a 'general stoppage of work in the Rhondda' was threatened. On the appointed day the situation was officially described as 'extremely delicate'. The leaders of the local medical aid society were thought to be 'quite capable of engineering street corner meetings for the purpose of bringing about a breakdown of the NHS'—and had threatened to do so. As a result, the societies were allowed to continue functioning a little longer. By 6 July a meeting of all doctors in the Rhondda had been held. Most decided to conform. One doctor at Llwynpia who practised a mile from the nearest chemist decided to continue dispensing until a (planned) branch of Boots was opened. And Dr Williams of the Tonypandy central surgery told his patients to have their prescriptions dispensed by a chemist if they wished, or by the medical aid society dispenser, who was qualified as a dispenser but not as a pharmacist. The latter arrangement contravened the National Health Service Act.[22]

The standard retort to these findings from NHS partisans would doubtless be that they were 'only' teething problems. But the important point is that there was no need to have created teething problems at all. The people of the Welsh valleys had created, and sustained and managed over many years, arrangements which suited them. It was within their power to improve those arrangements as they saw fit, as they had consistently done over many decades.

The experience described serves to illustrate a general truth about large-scale, comprehensive and compulsory social engineering: that the social engineers are irremediably ignorant. We may assume that Bevan's intentions towards the people of South Wales were benevolent. Yet he remained ignorant of the real effects the NHS was about to have (not only in South Wales generally but in his own constituency) until less than a month before the inauguration of the NHS. For a few days, after the facts were brought home to him, he acted decisively. Then he succumbed to the arguments of his officials.

The Fate Of The Medical Institutes In England

On the eve of the NHS in June 1948, there were 31 medical institutes

119

in England. Of these, 17 were to be taken over by existing medical officers on 5 July; in four instances the county councils were planning to take them over to run as health centres; in one case, York, the future was uncertain; and in nine instances the buildings were no longer to be used by GPs.[23]

The four premises to be taken over by county councils for use as health centres belonged to the former Luton Friendly Societies Medical Institute, the Great Western Railway Medical Fund Society of Swindon, the Gloucester Friendly Societies Medical Alliance, and the Gloucester Provident Dispensary.[24]

The health centres, which were expected to be in the forefront of NHS primary care, took a long time to materialise. By 1959 only 10 had been built.[25] In May 1966, after 18 years of the NHS, only 24 health centres had come into existence, although an additional 24 had been approved and were under construction.[26] Since then numbers have increased rapidly. Twenty years after the Act, however, there were *fewer* health centres than there had been medical institutes before 1946.

Conclusion

Before 1948 friendly society medical institutes and medical aid societies provided much-needed competition in the supply of medical care. This helped to contain prices in the non-government sector. Perhaps more significant was the innovative role of medical institutes and medical aid societies. As Aneurin Bevan acknowledged, they had pioneered new services which it was hoped the NHS would make standard. Yet, under the illusion that the political process can provide for innovation as effectively as the market, all alternatives to the NHS monolith were excluded. Due partly to government efforts to satiate professional demands, but also to a misguided faith in the omniscience and organisational capacity of government, the final vestiges of competition in the supply of health care were driven out of existence.

11

Re-Energising Civil Society

This final chapter turns to practical matters, concentrating on the reform of the welfare state. I offer three sets of proposals and three case studies. The first proposal emphasises the importance of subordinating politicians and public officials to the law. The second lists criteria for identifying responsibilities of the state consistent with liberty and questions the effectiveness of majority consent as a method of limiting the abuse of the powers of government. The third examines the personal values on which liberty rests, with special attention to the central role of the family in moulding men and women equipped for a free society. Finally, the three case studies of the application of civic capitalism are: health, education and protection of the poor.

1. De-Politicising the Law-Making Process

The most urgent task is to refresh our understanding of the ideal of liberty under law. Hayek's contribution was to show that the first liberal-democratic experiment failed because the institutions chosen by classical liberals to preserve liberty proved inadequate. Early classical liberals put their faith in the separation of powers—legislative, judicial and executive—but the separation was never fully achieved. The most sophisticated experiment, the American constitution, which was based on the division of power between the federal government and the states as well as the separation of federal powers, failed to contain central power because law-making was not sufficiently separated from policy-making. The Supreme Court was intended to check the politicisation of law-making but it too became politicised.

The remedy, argued Hayek, was to put the law above government. Earlier institutions did not work because classical-liberal thinkers were insufficiently on their guard against the perversion of the law-making process by politics. Most law in the seventeenth and eighteenth centuries was common law. Judges or scholars discovered it, they did not make it. The idea that the law was above interference by mere governments derived in part from the much earlier view that the law was God's law. It was taken for granted that no mere person or mere government could alter God's law. It is difficult for us today to understand that the law of the land was seen in the same light as God's law. But this was the view taken by the early liberals: no mere government could be allowed to interfere with law because it was the very means of limiting the abuses of rulers. Here Hayek's concern was similar to Oakeshott's. In a society of civil associates the law must not be the instrument of special interests, nor the tool of government. It must be that body of moral and prudential rules which is binding on everyone.

How can law-making be restored as an exercise in the making of the impartial rules of just conduct? Hayek's answer is that law-making in this special sense should be the task of a separate assembly. Historically Britain's mistake was to have allowed the same assembly that voted taxes also to make laws. Law-making is too important to be so determined. It requires a different temper, an impartial spirit, and a degree of wisdom, of which no hot-house political assembly is capable.

The mechanism proposed by Hayek for achieving a non-sectional state follows the practice of the ancient Athenians, a method also recommended by J.S. Mill.[1] In Athens at the height of the democratic period, the popular assembly could only pass decrees on particular matters of policy. A separate assembly, the *Nomothetae*, was charged with revising the laws, understood as rules of just conduct or *nomos*. In order to separate the promulgation of decrees dealing with particular matters from the making of rules of just conduct, Hayek suggested the establishment of *two* new popular assemblies: one charged with governing in the sense of carrying out a programme of work, and the other charged with formulating the *nomos*. He believed that people would choose very different representatives for the two assemblies:

> In choosing somebody most likely to look effectively after their particular interests and in choosing persons whom they can trust to uphold justice impartially the people would probably elect very different persons: effectiveness in the first kind of task demands qualities very different from the probity, wisdom, and judgement which are of prime importance in the second.

Hayek also suggested a device by which members of the legislative assembly could be protected from party discipline and from the fear of being penniless once their term of office had been completed, a vital safeguard if they are to be unflinchingly impartial. He proposed that everyone reaching the age of 45 in a given calender year should have a vote for candidates in the same age group, whose term of office would be fifteen years. The result would be an assembly of persons aged between 45 and 60, one-fifteenth of whom would retire every year.[2] As yet, Hayek's efforts to encourage the depoliticisation of law making have received scant attention and today's new laws continue to be more like political commands than moral rules.

Hayek's specific proposal may not be the best answer, but the deficiencies of his detailed scheme, should not diminish the importance of his main insight, that liberty rests on impartial law and is undermined when law serves sectional interests.

2. The Tasks of the State and the Province of the People: Where to Draw the Line

In addition to its role as maker and enforcer of the impartial rules of just conduct, the state is also useful because it can levy taxes to provide useful common services. This power, however, can be abused especially if the only limitation is that the government must secure majority support. Can some guiding principles be defined to assist taxpayers in deciding whether proposed government services are properly the province of the state?

Some counsel has been given by J.S. Mill, and the debate did not progress much until Hayek revived interest in the 1950s. Mill distinguished between the 'authoritative' and 'non-authoritative' activities of government.[3] Authoritative actions involved possible punishment, whereas non-authoritative actions did not. Mill gave three reasons for limiting non-authoritative state services. First, when private individuals could provide a better service the state should not be involved. Second, even if government officers could do a better job, there was still a presumption in favour of private provision as a means of educating people in the skills of voluntary co-operation. And third, there was a general presumption against adding too much to the government's powers, because the bigger it got, the greater its potential for harm. Hayek developed Mill's thinking. First he rejected *laissez-faire*:

The habitual appeal to the principle of non-interference in the fight against all ill-considered or harmful measures has had the effect of blurring the fundamental distinction between the kinds of measures which are and those which are not compatible with a free system.

It is, for Hayek, 'the character rather than the volume of government activity that is important'.[4] Above all, governments should not seek to bring about a given end result. They may prohibit harmful actions by law and they may provide services in order to widen the means available to private individuals. But they must not treat citizens as the means to an end desired by the authorities. The doctrine of the rule of law, according to Hayek, was intended to deny governments the method of specific orders or prohibitions directed at known persons. It did so in the hope of maximising the openings available to private individuals. But it was not intended to prevent governments from providing services which widened the scope of free citizens.

Some do not find this approach sufficiently distinct, arguing that because it enables no clear line to be 'drawn in the sand', the powers of government will tend to go on expanding. No one, however, has yet suggested a principle which provides the sought-after finality. Arthur Seldon, the intellectual inspiration of the IEA, suggests that 'the duties of government be confined to 'unavoidably collective functions',[5] or that government 'shall only do what cannot be done in the market'.[6] All such formulations leave an element of judgement.

As John Gray has recognised in *The Moral Foundations of Market Institutions*, no permanent principle circumscribing the scope of the state can be stated. We must, therefore, seek not a timeless binding axiom, but a guiding principle which accepts that we start on a given day, with the government as it is, armed only with a rule which helps us to decide in which direction to move. This brute reality was also fully recognised by Hayek.

For him, the first concern was that governments should not destroy the primary means which enable individuals to control their affairs. Consequently, governments should never control prices, access to occupations, the terms of sale and the amounts of a product to be made or sold. The test is whether the government is *providing means* for people to use their judgement in pursuit of their own goals or whether it is *using* people *as means* to ends of the government's devising. For instance, the government can properly require people entering an occupation to have acquired a given qualification, but only so long as everyone so qualified has a legal right to practise. To require followers of an occupation to obtain a qualification increases their knowledge and tells consumers something about them. It therefore increases the potential for progress. But to control access to an occupation leads to monopoly, favouritism and the suppression of the potential for creativity and initiative. Hayek also absolutely rules out the redistribution of wealth or income because it is incompatible with the free exercise of talent. But given these exclusions, a great deal of government action is still permissible.

Other measures may also be ruled out, argues Hayek, but only on grounds of expediency. In such cases, the main consideration will be whether the cost justifies the benefit. There are some services, for instance, which will not be provided by competitive enterprise because it is not possible or too difficult to charge beneficiaries. This category might include some public health measures and some roads. For the government to provide them would supplement private activity and create new means at the disposal of talented individuals and associations.

However, the manner in which such services are provided may also infringe liberty. There are two main concerns: the granting of monopoly and the establishment of administrative discretion. The first principle is that the state should never give itself a monopoly. Except in its role as upholder of the law, it should in all other respects operate on the same basis as everyone else.[7] However, the stipulation that the government must act as if it were a private person is not easy to enforce because taxes can readily be used to create a *de facto* monopoly. Constant vigilance is necessary.

Second, administrative discretion should be avoided. A free system does not rule out regulations applying equally to all, such as building regulations and factory legislation. The costs may outweigh the benefits, and the costs may be hidden, but such rules do not necessarily infringe liberty so long as they apply equally to all. People still interact as civil associates.[8]

A requirement, for instance, that all new brick buildings must be erected with a stipulated number of metal wall ties per square metre of brickwork (to bind the two brick walls together in a cavity wall) does not infringe liberty. Such a rule may be justified because once a house has been built the buyer cannot detect how many wall ties have been used without dismantling the wall. The building regulation creates confidence in building standards, saves buyers' time and allows them to use their energy more productively. It is an aid to the buyer. The added cost does not infringe liberty so long as all builders must comply. But if officials were empowered to pick and choose which houses they would require to be built with a certain number of wall ties, there would be a potential for abuse. They would be able to bias the prospects of some builders at the expense of others. The builders, that is, would have become mere means in the pursuit of the ends of the authorities.

It is true that when a rule applies equally to all, the government is telling people how to spend their own money, but such compulsion is permissible so long as its intention is to protect everyone from being deceived. Its primary intention and its outcome is to make voluntary co-operation more easy. The dividing line, therefore, is not between compulsion and non-compulsion, but between compulsion which results in releasing the maximum number of unknown people to use their own knowledge in their own way, thus increasing the potential for progress; and compulsion which, because it is directed against people favoured or disfavoured by the authorities, results in the government selecting who will be able to contribute their full potential to human advance. By imposing many regulations adding to the cost of building, the people within a nation may be rendered incapable of competing with citizens of other countries. But in Hayek's terminology, such imposition would be inexpedient; it would not infringe liberty.

Civic capitalists have argued that if human civilisation is to flourish we need to allow room for the growth of human understanding. We can never know the future state of our knowledge, and we can never know beforehand who the great benefactors of humankind will be. Consequently we must permit all to back their own beliefs at their own risk, revealing through trial and error who will make the discoveries and produce the ideas that improve the human condition.

This necessity to allow for the growth of human understanding is the chief reason why civic capitalists feared government provision of services, particularly monopoly provision. At any given state of our knowledge a government monopoly may be capable of providing a limited, given level of service effectively. But such an arrangement, if it suppresses alternatives, will stifle change and obstruct progress and thus impede the very means by which we can provide still better services than we can currently imagine. This tendency to cause stagnation was the flaw in communism, and it is the flaw in milder types of collectivism. When the yoke of communist government was removed from Eastern Europe towards the end of 1989, it was commonly remarked that communism had made few improvements in people's lives. It had lived off the physical capital and the human skills which European civilisation had created over previous centuries. The purpose of government committed to liberty is to create the growing room in which human initiative, energy and creativity can bring about improvements for all.

A 'Necessity Audit'

Which tasks are appropriate for the state? If Hayek was right, we should submit present public-sector services to tests of their necessity. This might be accomplished by subjecting every existing government activity (or proposal for new activity) to a 'necessity audit', to establish whether it belongs in the public sector or not. But we must be clear about the reasons for questioning public-sector provision. It is not enough to proffer a general inclination for non-intervention, or *laissez-faire*, or 'small government'. The fundamental question is this: Is the government using its powers to direct the energies of its people to a given end? That is to say: is the government *using* people *as* means; or is it *providing* them *with* means? If the purpose of government is not to replace private initiative, but to support and complement it then, following Mill and Hayek, we might usefully direct five questions at existing government services.

1. Could a better service be provided by private associations? If yes, why is it in the public sector at all?

2. Even if the government can provide the service more efficiently, is there a case for putting it in the private sector as a means of improving through experience the 'moral, intellectual and active' qualities of the people?

3. Where there is a case for state provision, does the state have a monopoly? If it does, then it will suppress the new initiatives on which progress depends. Services improve through experimentation, which provokes new ideas which can be emulated if they are admired, or rejected if disliked. Any monopoly, and particularly a public-sector monopoly, suppresses the diversity on which progress depends.

4. Where there is a case for state provision, can administrative discretion be avoided? The wider the discretion, the greater the potential for abuse.

5. Where there is a case for public-sector provision, does the service need to be provided by central government or could it be provided by local government?

Local or Central Government?

As a general rule, wherever possible, services which belong in the public sector should be supplied locally by self-financing units of government. There can be no absolute right answer about the necessity for a service to be public or private, or publicly financed yet privately provided, and consequently we should allow room for different localities to experiment, some with more or less public services, others with direct provision, and still others with local finance combined with competitive tendering by private agencies. But units of local government should experiment at their own cost. This would mean financing local government from local taxes without any subsidy from general taxes whatsoever, so that local decisions are made by cost-conscious taxpayers on their own behalf. Among the weaknesses of the ill-judged poll tax was its failure to remove central subsidies, thus leaving taxpayers unaware of exactly how much local public services were costing them. It is fundamental to liberty that people should be free to say yes or no to taxation and without full information about the services they are receiving in return for their taxes it is impossible to form a rational judgement.[9]

Because the cost-consciousness of local taxpayers has been weakened by cross-subsidies from general taxes, British local government has become in large measure an arm of central government. Similarly, American states through federal subsidies have become instruments of federal power, though to a lesser degree than British local authorities.

Local government is advantageous, not only because it allows taxpayers to be more aware of the cost, but also because it allows small-scale experimentation, which means that when things go wrong mistakes can be detected early and corrected before too much harm is done. The more complex and extensive the experiment, the greater is the risk of serious harm. In this respect there is much common ground between social democrats and Hayek. Sir Karl Popper, for instance, long retained considerable sympathy for social democracy, but he was severe in his warnings about the dangers of statist experiments. Social engineering, he argued, should be conducted on a small scale and the results carefully monitored to allow for the correction of errors.[10]

The Burden of Proof

The presumption in devising public policies should be against public-sector provision, and above all against monopoly. Those who want a given service to be in the public sector must accept the burden of proof. They must show either that the service would not be provided at all if the government did not provide it, or that it could be supplied more efficiently by the government. Even if a proposal can pass the test of superior efficiency there is still a presumption in favour of private provision as a means of widening opportunities for acquiring the personal skills necessary in a free and democratic society. And when there is a case for public-sector provision, the first resort should be provision by local authorities competing with each other for population.

If these principles were applied then wide scope would be allowed for the emergence of voluntary associations to meet the many needs of fellow citizens. And as the historical record amply demonstrates, voluntarism not only offered superior quality services but also provided opportunities for developing the personal skills necessary for liberty. It is only if such opportunities are widely available that freedom can be made safe from tyranny. The importance of providing opportunities to improve the character of the people can be seen with special clarity in Eastern Europe, where it is the key to the reconstruction of civil society on the ruins of communism. The pre-1989 dictatorships preferred pliable drones to strong characters, but people who have become self-confident through success in providing services for the good of their fellows will not readily submit to any future totalitarian offering.

3. A Morality For Liberty

One of the paradoxes of the age is that opinion leaders harbour moral doubts about capitalism despite its overwhelming success in enabling men and women to create unprecedented prosperity and thus to release millions from the immediate pressures of survival to concentrate on better things. The people of countries which have not adopted liberty as their watchword—still the great majority of the world's population—live out their days dominated by the hard slog of making ends meet. The chief rival to capitalism, communism, has failed and is no longer considered a serious alternative.

Sometimes moral doubts about capitalism—shorthand for the free way of life we enjoy in the West—are the doubts of authoritarians who would abandon freedom for some new version of state socialism. But the mentality of die-hard socialists does not account in full for the wide suspicion of capitalism. The chief reason is a deep mistrust of an excessively materialistic philosophy which fails to appeal to the best in people. Most people want prosperity, and they are not ashamed of wanting it. But it is not all they want. The British are heirs to a profound civilisation and find it difficult to give their hearts to a creed which seems to regard prosperity as the ultimate end of life.

Labour's failure at the last General Election provides support for this interpretation. Moral doubts about capitalist materialism have been exploited by socialists who present themselves as offering a more 'caring' society. Yet, in practice, socialism is equally materialistic, for it turns out that its moral vision has to do with money and little else. The gut feeling that drives its activists is the passion for material equality. They define equality as enforced equal (or more equal) spending power. But their aspiration does not appeal to most Britons.

It seems that the British people harbour values which are not fully articulated, of which they are not fully conscious, and which neverthe-less guide their conduct at election time? How much commitment is there to the traditional civic virtues—such as honesty, duty, self-sacrifice, honour, service, self-discipline, self-improvement, civility, fortitude, courage, diligence and patriotism—which appeal to our better nature?

The attack on traditional values began in earnest in the 1960s. People raised before then have long memories, and there is a dialogue between the generations. There are also many still alive who experienced the self-sacrifice of the last war, risking their own lives out of love for their country. They did not love their country because they supported it 'right or wrong', but because their country was the guardian of liberty and was fighting a just war against a wicked tyranny.

Despite the efforts of a minority of school teachers to dismiss past heroes, many of the young can still share the emotions of the sailors who, as they manned their cannons before the battle of Trafalgar, were stirred by Nelson's signal: 'England expects every man will do his duty'. Nelson had no need of more words. He could count on the courage, application and moral qualities of his men.

It is true that the young read less, but the books of England's literary past are still available, and still being read, reminding readers of the values traditionally celebrated in this land. Popular culture is often said to have undermined traditional values, and so it has to some extent. But popular culture does not only celebrate nihilism. In Clint Eastwood's 'Dirty Harry' films, for instance, the hero is on the side of traditional values. A punk is a punk, whether or not he came from a difficult neighbourhood, and he will assuredly be on the receiving end of Eastwood's righteous violence. Violence is glorified, but it is the anti-social punk who suffers.

Television is often blamed, but its influence is not uni-directional. The period dramas, for which British television is noted, often manage to portray the good character, sobriety, self-improvement, and self-discipline of our forbears, reminding us why only fifty years ago men and women considered their country worth dying for.

Britain remains an open society, and despite the best efforts of the chattering classes, enough people receive enough exposure to traditional values to keep them alive both in memory and in practice. This fact was the deep spring that Mrs Thatcher tapped and explains why a woman who in public lacked the warmth to be personally likeable, and who was not much liked, nevertheless was popular. She reminded Britons of their past, and told them that the essential British character was strong, and that to have become the 'sick man of Europe' was not in our nature. It was the result of a mistaken departure from the values and institutions which had stood us in good stead for centuries.

The wish to restore traditional values was part of Thatcherism and goes some way to explaining its success. But there was another side to the thinking of the 1980s which explains why the Thatcherite revolution was ultimately built on sand. Its language was too materialistic, that is, too guided by the peculiar materialism of a particular school of economic theory which sees people as 'utility maximisers', that is maximisers of their satisfactions. This model can be a useful explanatory tool in accounting for some (by no means all) business behaviour, but it cannot account for liberty and it does not embrace the full gamut of ideals, passions, motives, duties, hopes, doubts and fears which are the reality of life.

The reforms that dominated late Thatcherism exemplify the malaise. For the lover of liberty the real problem with the NHS is that the state treats people as if they were children, who must be protected from all cares, ostensibly free of charge but actually out of their own pockets. For the civic capitalist, the reform strategy should therefore have sought to restore personal responsibility for health care, with the state concentrating on protection of the poor (as outlined below). But the government did not define the problem that way. It wanted primarily to secure value for money and consequently imposed an internal market.

Consider also the Thatcher education reforms. The real problem is that the welfare state has stripped parents of a major part of the responsibility for raising their own children and thus helped to undermine the family, the main building block of a free society. The government, however, was guided in part by socialist mistrust of parents—who, they thought, would probably make unwise choices —but also by a shallow view of human nature. It used the rhetoric of consumerism and sought to make money follow the parents' choice. But it did not speak of restoring responsibility to parents, and did not appeal to the special bond between parents and their own children in order to harness their powerful enthusiasm in shaking up our schools.

The ideal of liberty ranges far beyond the market. Historically its supporters wanted to create and foster institutions that would encourage self-improvement. When, in the middle of the nineteenth century, its chief defenders made *laissez faire* the heart of their philosophy and portrayed people primarily as satisfaction seekers, liberty lost its moral force. And it has yet to retrieve it.

There are some free marketeers who are doubtful about this line of reasoning. For instance, when I suggested to one economist that market philosophy had been only partially successful in the 1980s because it appeared to have no ethos of personal responsibility and no commitment to moral self-improvement, he remarked, 'Wasn't that what George Blake (the British communist traitor) said about communism?' Blake apparently felt that communism could have worked if only people had improved enough. But the civic capitalists of history did not hope to create 'new men'. They set out to inspire people, whereas communists began by forcing people to conform to their ideals and were quick to assume innate wickedness on the part of people who did not toe the line, thus providing a rationale for cruelty or killing.

Civic capitalists always understood that life is a perpetual struggle against imperfection. They did not expect perfection to be achieved. And they saw moral improvement as a strictly voluntary process. To force people to be better was a contradiction in terms, for to be a better person was precisely to improve despite temptations. It is true that communists repeatedly disguised the squalid coercion of their rule by professing high ideals, a strategy which successfully deceived many Western intellectuals. It is also true that idealists have often resorted to force to make people change. But it is a fundamental error to associate all idealism with coercion. The difference is between those who, on the one hand, expect perfection here on Earth and who therefore believe in the perfectibility of man; and those who, on the other, aspire to perfection as a useful ultimate target but who are never surprised when people fall short of the ideal and who react to imperfection, not with anger and punishment, but with initial sorrow followed promptly by dogged renewal of the struggle for voluntary improvement.

Some free marketeers, the hard-boiled economic rationalists, have fallen into the trap of seeing all high moral talk as a prelude to state coercion. But in doing so they are failing to do justice to the tradition of thought to which they belong. Liberty was always that combination of institutions which saw life as a struggle against human imperfection. The law was the backstop, threatening wrongdoers with punishment in narrowly defined cases. Competition served to channel possibly selfish energies into the service of others, and the moral environment rested in part on the sanction of disapproval, but above all on everyone sharing in the endeavour of encouraging others to behave in a just and considerate manner. It was understood that maintaining a moral climate required constant effort, just as the swimmer who hopes to avoid sinking like a stone will find it easier to stay afloat if he keeps moving. There is no end, not at least in this world.

To view people as utility maximisers and to erect public policies on this presumption is to build on sand. The free way of life we have enjoyed in the West rests on avoiding concentrations of power. It works best when the power thus dispersed inspires the efforts of people equipped to use it. If people see themselves only as satisfaction seekers, maximising their advantages, they will dream only small dreams and the system will wither. It may survive, as Adam Smith recognised, for much can be accomplished by each of us seeking his mutual advantage in a competitive system. But it would be a poor society if the highest ideal was mutual gain. We each have larger and more generous instincts.

The Family

The family has traditionally been regarded as the foundation stone of a free society. It is in the family that people first learn the self-restraint and consideration for others on which a tolerant, free and democratic society rests. Recently, however, there have been signs of a weakening of family life. There has been a sharp increase in the number of one-parent families. They now comprise about one fifth of all families. A major factor has been the rise in illegitimate births from 5 per cent in 1947 to 30 per cent in 1991, but the biggest single cause has been the growth in divorce and separation. Some 63 per cent of lone mothers have been divorced or separated, 29 per cent have never-married (including co-habiting couples), and eight per cent are widows.

Until recently it was taken for granted that if youngsters were to stand a good chance of growing into responsible adults in a free and stable society they would need the constant guidance of two com-mitted parents, wherever possible, assisted by the grandparents and aunts and uncles of the extended family. Today this view is no longer fully accepted. Not every one-parent family is a problem: there are examples of heroic and successful lone parents and there are inadequate two-parent families. But research consistently confirms that, on average, the children of single parents do less well in school, are more likely to turn to crime, and develop less well physically.[11] Awareness of the gravity of the problem is shared across the political spectrum and one of the finest discussions has been produced by authors with socialist sympathies, *Families Without Fatherhood*, by Norman Dennis and George Erdos with an introduction by the doyen of democratic socialists, Professor A.H. Halsey.[12]

Liberty is associated with lifestyle choice, but this cannot mean that every duty can be abandoned at will. If a man and a woman bring a child into the world it is not unreasonable to expect them to look after the child until he or she is grown up. To choose not to do so cannot be seen as a legitimate lifestyle choice. Some public discussion implies that it is authoritarian to insist on parents looking after their children until they reach adulthood. But if, as I contend, liberty depends on the free acceptance of some basic duties, then the obligation to be a devoted mother and father to your own children is surely one of them. On such fundamental issues confusion currently reigns.

Historically, civic capitalists have taken the view that marriage is not merely a choice but a commitment, that is a solemn promise made in the presence of family, friends and the authorities to support each other and any children that may follow. To restore this understanding of marriage as a commitment does not mean the restoration of male-dominated families, nor that women must never go out to work. Marriage has become a more equal partnership, and rightly so, and there is no reason why mothers cannot work while their children are at school, especially when one income is insufficient to support the children. But if marriage is a mere 'convenience for the time being' it cannot perform its unique task of raising citizens equipped for freedom.[13]

The value to a free society of marriage-as-a-commitment is that children acquire from their parents the capacity for self-sacrifice and duty. They acquire it by copying the conduct of their parents and especially that of their mother. Liberty is in this sense built on the unconditional love of mothers for their children. But if the parents put their own interests first, they can hardly teach their children the virtue of considering others. Joseph Schumpeter warned from the 1940s onwards of the danger to a free society of undermining the family. The question in many parents' minds was, he said: 'Why should we stunt our ambitions and impoverish our lives in order to be insulted and looked down upon in our old age'.[14] If this question becomes paramount in the minds of most parents the family will not last long.

Liberty rests on some institutions, habits, values and dispositions being seen as sacred. Some free marketeers and many on the left would mock any such claim, but as the founding father of the Chicago school of economists, Frank Knight, convincingly argued, classical liberalism has always had its sacred, untouchable elements of which private property is the foremost.[15] For liberty to be safe, should the idea of marriage as a commitment be given the same sacred standing?

The Social Market Economy

Before turning to the case studies it may be advisable to avoid a possible source of confusion. Among the critics of Thatcherism are enthusiasts for the social market, and it is true that the approach advocated in *Reinventing Civil Society* shares common ground with the social-market view, at least in its support for market competition. However, there are significant differences.

In common parlance the term 'social market' has come to mean little more than 'capitalism plus a substantial welfare state', involving unfunded benefits, the deliberate redistribution of incomes and the imposition of social benefits on employers to the detriment of employment prospects. Plainly this tradition is inconsistent with one of the central concerns of the view I have been calling civic capitalism, namely the crowding out of civil society by the welfare state. Advocates of what might be called the 'street' version of the social market attach insufficient, if any, weight to this problem.

However, there is an older tradition of the social market economy which has much in common with civic capitalism. It is the tradition of the 'Ordo' group of liberals who set out to build a genuinely free society on the ruins of Hitler's Germany. The group, named after its journal *Ordo: Jahrbuch für die Ordnung von Wirtschaft und Gesellschaft*, included Walter Eucken, Wilhelm Röpke and Ludwig Erhard, Germany's first post-war economics minister. As Norman Barry has shown, members of the Ordo group belong in the classical-liberal tradition, but did not agree with the view of many economists that the market was self-correcting. In particular, they saw industrial monopoly as a constant danger.[16] They were critical of *laissez-faire* economics and believed that freedom rested, not on markets alone but on a well-constructed system of law and morals. Eucken, for instance, argued that: 'the economic system cannot be left to organise itself. So there is no question of any return to *laissez faire*'.[17] As the passages quoted earlier showed, both Adam Smith (above p. 16) and Hayek (above p. 19) took a similar line.

However, the Ordo-liberals were as sceptical about the redistributive state as about *laissez-faire* capitalism. They had no hesitation in expecting the state to assist the casualties of a market economy, but they did not support the welfarism that had been a feature of German life since Bismarck.[18]

Thus, the tradition of the Ordo-liberals shares common ground with civic capitalism, but today the term 'social market' does not mean the Ordo-liberalism of Röpke, Eucken and Erhard, rather it means welfare capitalism. And in the 1990s we can now see how the welfare state destroys the fabric and richness of civil society by cramping the space available for personal idealism.

Case Studies

It is not the intention of this book to produce a full-fledged pro-gramme of reform. Instead, I have tried to suggest the general direction of reform in health, education and the relief of poverty. These services have been chosen because for many people they are the undeniable province of the state. I challenge that view.

Before turning to these services, a word about industrial monop-oly may be advisable. I have emphasised that civic capitalists wished to avoid concentrations of power, but one of the socialist criticisms of market societies is that markets tend to monopoly. This tendency is much exaggerated but it cannot be denied that monopolies do emerge. The 'textbook' reply is that monopolies are self-correcting and that they only remain entrenched when governments intervene on their behalf to secure the monopoly. This counter view is supported by much evidence, but there will undoubtedly be periods, perhaps long periods, when consumers will have to tolerate a monopoly in the supply of a particular product. The textbook answer is that consumers should learn to wait for the market to correct itself because state action may produce an even worse result. Again, this view has much force but for many it is too complacent. This is why I share Hayek's view in *The Constitution of Liberty* that 'it may be a good thing if the monopolist is treated as a sort of whipping boy of economic policy', as we have seen above, so long as enforcement is confined to the application of general rules and no agents of government are permitted to enjoy administrative discretion.[19]

Now it is time to raise again the importance of avoiding govern-ment monopolies, and to revisit the question of 'necessity audits'.

The Education System

Consider how the education system would survive a necessity audit. First, can education be provided privately? Indeed it can, and after many years of concern about declining standards in state schools few can doubt the relative efficiency of private schools. Second, does the present system suppress opportunities for the development of moral, intellectual and active qualities? There can be no better example of how, if the state does too much, it narrows the scope for personal idealism and achievement. In education the parents' responsibility has been severely narrowed.

Third, state education in Britain is a system of local monopolies. The government's education reforms have been contradictory. Some measures, such as the local management of schools, have encouraged decentralisation; others work in the opposite direction, particularly the national curriculum. The principal weakness of the national curriculum is that it suppresses differences between schools and reduces choice. It also reduces the chances of rejuvenating the teaching profession, which has fallen prey to a shallow, trade-union mentality.

A reform strategy for education should have two main aims: (1) it should seek to restore parental responsibility by reducing taxes to allow parents to spend their own money on educating their own children; and (2) it should seek to de-regulate the supply side to encourage the founding of new schools and break the power of local public-sector monopolies.

First, on the demand side parents should be empowered so that their choices count. The family remains the best institution for raising children to become men and women of good character. The ethos of the school should not, therefore, contradict the authority of parents. Indeed, schooling should be seen as an extension of the family. The only certain way to ensure that the family and the school work in partnership is for the parents to be free to choose their school and switch to another when they wish. This is only possible if the school relies on parents for their income, and this means parental payment. Without it, there will be no effective accountability. Payment will allow parents to choose schools which do not concentrate on academic work alone and which also give a moral lead in partnership with the home.

Historically, classical liberals have argued that the empowerment of parents should be achieved through a voucher scheme, under which we would all pay for education through taxes and receive back from the state a voucher which could be exchanged at any school in return for the education of a child. A better alternative would be to restore to parents the spending power confiscated by the Inland Revenue, so that most would be able to pay for their own children's education. The state should accept responsibility for the poorest children so that all enjoy the opportunity to be educated.

In addition to demand-side empowerment, radical supply-side de-regulation to break the stranglehold of central authority and to re-energise the idealism of teachers is also necessary. It would not be enough to transform all state schools into grant maintained schools, as some have proposed, even though the result would be the abolition of local education authorities. This approach might yield considerable benefits, but it would fail sufficiently to de-regulate the supply side. It is now well established that the key to the successful functioning of any market is the possibility that new entrants will take market share from existing schools. Without this discipline, established providers too easily settle down to a cosy co-existence.

Ultimately, all schools should be private. Teachers or others should be free to found new schools, and it should be possible for existing state schools to become private. Schools would then have total control of admissions, school numbers, governing structure, teacher tenure, training and salaries. They would set their own fees and they would not be accountable for their performance to any higher authority, other than parents. Neither the central government nor local authorities would have power over schools.

Radical de-regulation would help to re-energise teachers and re-activate dormant parental responsibility and commitment. The Government's approach to teachers has been to impose the national curriculum in the hope of stipulating from Whitehall what should happen in each classroom. But laying down guidelines from on high is unlikely to harness the commitment of teachers. It is true that some teachers are hopeless ideologues unfit to be in charge of the young, but this is not true of the majority, and unless their good will is harnessed Britain's schools will not flourish. A policy of de-regulation will allow new schools to be founded built around teacher commit-ment where it exists. This approach would be especially advantageous in inner-city areas because it would permit teachers with a special sense of mission to assist the poor by founding new schools.

The Thatcher and Major Governments have both used the rhetoric of consumer choice which, at first glance, gives the impression that their policy resembles the one advocated here. But the difference is that the primary aim of recent governments has not been to repair the dormant home-school partnership by bringing home and school together. Instead it has been based on a division between the school and the home with the parents seen as outsiders standing in judgement of schools. The 1988 education reforms turn out to have been another example of the consequences of working with a restricted view of the market. Parents were permitted a choice of school (highly constrained by the availability of places) as an instrument of central government policy. But what is valuable about the free association of people in a competitive market is, not only that many groups are free to use assets as they believe best, but also that people are free to improve their personal qualities and skills under the stimulus of competition. The free employment of human ingenuity and human idealism, 'human capital' to speak more technically, is the essence of a free market.[20] The tendency of the Thatcher and Major Governments, however, has not been to widen the scope for human creativity, but to increase central control. This emphasis has been their undoing for, to implement their reforms, it has forced them to rely heavily on teachers. If they had sought to disperse power to parents who in their turn can be expected to forge partnerships with schools, the confrontation over the national curriculum tests and the publication of results could have been avoided and the foundations laid for improved schooling for all.

The experiment in East Harlem, begun in the early 1970s showed the striking benefits that de-regulation can yield. In 1973, out of 32 school districts in New York, East Harlem was last in reading and maths. Poverty was widespread, with some 80 per cent of pupils receiving free lunches and more than half the families headed by lone females. The racial mix was 60 per cent Hispanic and 35 per cent black.

From 1974 the supply side was reformed. Teachers were encouraged to put forward their own proposals for new schools and instead of being centred on a building, schools were to be built around themes, programmes and philosophies. Each school had control of its own admissions and curriculum and parents enjoyed complete choice of school, with money following their choice. Parents were encouraged to participate in their school and to feel a real sense of ownership. No less important, when schools failed to attract pupils they were closed.

The scheme has functioned since 1974 and the results have been dramatic. Schools proliferated, specialising in a wide variety of subjects, as the following examples testify: the Academy of Environmental Science, the Creative Learning Community, East Harlem

Career Academy, East Harlem Maritime School, East Harlem School for Health and Biomedical Studies, the José Feliciano Performing Arts School, and the Isaac Newton School for Math and Science.

About 60 per cent of children received their first choice, 30 per cent their second choice, and five per cent their third choice. Student achievement improved. In 1973, only 16 per cent of pupils were reading at or above their grade level. In 1987, the figure was 63 per cent. By the end of the early 1990s East Harlem was in the middle of the performance range for New York's 32 districts. John Chubb and Terry Moe, the authors of an authoritative Brookings Institution study, *Politics, Markets and America's Schools*, concluded:

> On virtually every relevant dimension, the East Harlem reforms have been a tremendous success. There are lots of schools, emphasising everything from music to science. Teachers are enthusiastic about their work and largely in control of their own schools. They are empowered, professional, and satisfied—all achieved through the natural dynamics of the system, not through the artificiality of bureaucratic rules. School organisations are small and informal, built around team cooperation and coherence of mission. Parents are active, well informed, and take pride in 'their' schools.[21]

I am proposing to go further than the East Harlem reforms, but the approach adopted in that school district, despite limitations, promises to be a far more effective method of improving Britain's inner city schools than anything so far offered by recent British governments.

The NHS

How would the NHS withstand a 'necessity audit'? Could the service be provided more effectively by private enterprise? There is little doubt that it could, which is why most European countries have not copied the NHS and allow far more private hospital ownership. Does the state have a monopoly? The NHS is among the biggest public-sector monopolies ever. Does the state exercise unjustified discretion? Indeed it does, even to the point of withholding life-saving treatment.

Let's pretend for a moment that the NHS is based on insurance. If so, it is a type of insurance which allows the insurer to take random amounts of money without offering a contract for cover in return. In effect the insurance policy says, first, you must pay so much per year but we refuse to say how much. Second, we will just take the amount of our choosing out of your pay packet. And third we will promise only to give you the service we consider appropriate, you have no fixed entitlements. The 'right' to health care has turned out to be a command from the government instructing individuals to spend their own money on a public sector monopoly.

The great majority of people want essential medical care to be available to all, whether rich or poor, but what they have not understood is that the NHS is a very ineffective way of achieving this end. If the poor were protected by giving them purchasing power instead of services in kind they would be in a position to demand a more responsive service from the producers. And the great majority of the population could be left free to choose the sort of insurance policy they judge to be right for them. The NHS gives people what the medical authorities consider to be good for them, not what they would choose for themselves in the light of the cost and their personal preferences.

The objective of reform, therefore, should be to bring about private ownership of public-sector hospitals and to finance health care through private insurance, not taxation. It would be straightforward to privatise the hospitals, especially since most are now NHS trusts. Reforming the method of financing health care would be more difficult, not least because private insurance has its imperfections. But these can be overcome, as I have argued elsewhere.[22]

The best way of restoring personal responsibility for payment would be to enable individuals to contract out of the NHS, just as they can contract out of the state pension scheme. A fuller version of this proposal can be found in *Everyone a Private Patient* and what follows is only a summary.[23] No one would be forced to leave the NHS, but individuals who are dissatisfied would be free to claim back an age-weighted payment equivalent to what they have paid in taxes for health care. They would be obliged to take out health insurance covering the services currently made available under the NHS and to take out catastrophe cover, so that no one could find himself bankrupted by the cost of treatment. Initially NHS hospitals would provide accident and emergency cover.

People thus insured would be free to seek care from private hospitals or the NHS. If they used the NHS they would be charged and recover the cost from their insurer. Such a scheme would enable patients to insist on a better service and help to bring to an end the rationing which lies at the heart of the NHS. Above all, it would unleash the human ingenuity and idealism which is suppressed, though not fully stifled, by the NHS monopoly. One outcome could be the rejuvenation of the ethos of service that was typical of the pre-1948 voluntary hospitals. Indeed, the NHS has not so far fully destroyed that ethos and its continuation in some historic hospitals largely explains why the NHS is not uniformly bad. Perhaps organisations representing consumers, possibly resembling the old friendly societies, might re-emerge. We never know what the future may hold, but there is surely one clear lesson of past experience, namely that it is never wise to narrow the openings which allow people to do good in their own way.

The Relief of Poverty

What is the state's responsibility for the poor? No one should be allowed to starve or suffer severe privation. This principle is the minimum obligation we owe to one another as fellow members of the same nation. The sense of solidarity vital to mutual regard rests primarily on shared respect for the law, but also on the knowledge that we will not allow one of our number to fall below a certain threshold. The presence of the safety net should not be left to chance and governments are well placed to ensure that no one falls through it.

If it is a legitimate responsibility of the state to prevent people falling below a certain income threshold, then no government can escape considering how best to maintain this safety net without doing more harm than good.

The first danger is that the relief of poverty will be used as a cover for equalisation. I argued earlier that one of the guiding principles of a free society should be that the state should not *use* people *as means* to an end of the government's choosing, but that it may *provide* them with means. It has been put to me that this guiding principle does not rule out all compulsory transfers of cash because when a person is given money by the government it can be said that he is being given means. But there is a clear difference between, on the one hand, protecting people from falling below a standard of life which would make them incapable of making any use whatever of their talents, and on the other, seeking to make every person in the society conform to the government's view of the proper distribution of income and wealth. The latter involves the government using people to fit its own abstract scheme.

To accept that the state should maintain a safety net in order to prevent hardship, and thus the potential waste of talent, is quite different from urging that it should use its powers of compulsion to compress incomes until they conform to some pre-ordained pattern. The pursuit of equality of outcomes is not compatible with a liberal system because the pervasive apparatus inevitably required to bring it about concentrates power in too few hands. When a government pursues a policy of redistribution, we all become tools of the state. Moreover, the practical reality of pursuing equality during the post-war years has been the transfer of power, not from the rich to the poor, but from everyone, rich and poor alike, to the state.

Equalisation has also had a corrupting effect on the political process. It has become a battleground for benefits at other people's expense. Politicians are not expected to be principled makers of the laws necessary for the exercise of liberty, but brokers who offer to finance private advantages at the expense of the taxpayer. This tendency reinforces the inherent amorality of mass decision making. As James Madison pointed out at the time of the American constitutional debates, the trouble with politics is that it dilutes the effectiveness of conscience by increasing the number 'among whom the blame or praise is to be divided'. Conscience, he said, 'is known to be inadequate in individuals; in large numbers little is to be expected from it'.[24]

No less important, redistributive justice is represented as a moral ideal when it is no such thing. Throughout the history of Western civilisation morality has been seen as demanding much of the individual. Adam Smith recognised that we can achieve much by pursuing our legitimate self-interest through mutual adjustment to others, but he also thought that any worthy human being should seek to do right according to his sense of duty (above p. 26).

The allure of redistributive justice as an ideal is that it does not demand anything of its champions. Indeed its whole thrust is to demand contributions from *other* people, whether the rich or the taxpaying citizen. The goodness of people is measured by the vehemence with which they demand action by others, not their willingness to sacrifice themselves. Redistributive justice, therefore, fails to appeal to the best in people; on the contrary, it appeals to the selfish side of human nature.

Equality of opportunity is also a trap. It tends to mean equality at the 'starting gate', which implies hostility to the family. It is an inevitable and unavoidable element of the human condition to be born into a particular family and for some families to confer more advantages than others on their offspring. The egalitarian view tends to be that if good parents give a child a better start, the advantage gained is illegitimate because it is not the result of the child's own merit.

The second danger inherent in state relief of poverty is that a group of people will emerge who grow accustomed to life on income support. As J.S. Mill put it:

> in all cases of helping, there are two sets of consequences to be considered; the *consequences of the assistance itself*, and the consequences of *relying* on the assistance. The former are generally beneficial, but the latter, for the most part, injurious; so much so, in many cases, as greatly to outweigh the value of the benefit. (Emphasis added.)

This is never more likely to happen, he thought, than in the very cases where the need for help is the most intense. Mill also saw how and when help could be bracing:

> When the condition of any one is so disastrous that his energies are paralysed by discouragement, assistance is a tonic, not a sedative: it braces instead of deadening the active faculties; always provided that the assistance is not such as to dispense with self-help, by substituting itself for the person's own labour, skill and prudence, but is limited to affording him a better hope of attaining success by those legitimate means.

He recognises that:

> In so far as the subject admits of any general doctrine or maxim, it would appear to be this—that if assistance is given in such a manner that the condition of the person helped is as desirable as that of the person who succeeds in doing the same thing without help, the assistance, if capable of being previously calculated on, is mischievous: but if, while available to everybody, it leaves to every one a strong motive to do without it if he can, it is then for the most part beneficial.[25]

But, whilst he thought that the state should provide a guarantee for all, it was no less important that 'the task of distinguishing between one case of real necessity and another' should be the responsibility of private initiative. A private charity could give more to the deserving, whereas the state must act according to general rules. He also thought it wrong for public officials to distinguish between the deserving and the undeserving:

it would show much ignorance of the ways of mankind to suppose that such persons, even in the almost impossible case of their being qualified, will take the trouble of ascertaining and sifting the past conduct of a person in distress, so as to form a rational judgement on it. Private charity can make these distinctions; and in bestowing its own money, is entitled to do so according to its own judgement... But the administrators of a public fund ought not to be required to do more for anybody, than that minimum which is due even to the worst. If they are, the indulgence very speedily becomes the rule, and refusal the more or less capricious or tyrannical exception.[26]

The distinctive character of Mill's approach is that it treats poor people as moral agents, not as victims of circumstance. The dominant view for much of this century has been that people are poor because factors outside their control have brought them down. The general direction of public policy has therefore been to try out various programmes to act *upon* the poor. They are treated as passive victims who can be made to react to public policies. They are studied *en masse*, by analysing statistics which are often collected by the government for its own administrative purposes, not with the intention of understanding the poor. The effects of new policies are often studied in the same manner, from the outside looking in. The weakness of this approach is that it fails to take into account the single most important human quality, that we are all capable of moral and prudential choice and that our inner resources make a great difference to our lives. Public policy ought to bear this reality in mind.

A Proposal

Here are some possible means of developing a new approach aimed at restoring the dependent poor to independent citizenship. The underlying assumption is that practical help is superior to mere almsgiving, whether by charity or the state. Sending giro cheques is too easy. Real caring means time and trouble, not mere cash support. The purpose, therefore, is to give the able-bodied poor the opportunity to put something back, not only to spend.

The chief danger to be avoided is the 'crowding out' effect of the welfare state. As state welfare has grown so it has squeezed out voluntary associations and diminished the spirit of personal responsibility on which a vibrant civil society rests. Tocqueville, writing about emerging modern societies based on his visit to America in the 1830s, foresaw that the new social order might fall prey to an entirely novel type of despotism. His warning seems more apposite as each year passes. The root cause, he thought, was excessive individualism:

> The first thing that strikes the observation is an innumerable multitude of men, all equal and alike, incessantly endeavouring to procure the petty and paltry pleasures with which they glut their lives. Each of them, living apart, is as a stranger to the fate of all the rest; his children and his private friends constitute to him the whole of mankind. As for the rest of his fellow citizens, he is close to them, but he does not see them; he touches them, but he does not feel them; he exists only for himself and himself alone...

People of this character, warned Tocqueville, may come to be ruled by:

> an immense and tutelary power, which takes upon itself alone to secure their gratifications and to watch over their fate. That power is absolute, minute, regular, provident and mild. It would be like the authority of a parent if, like that authority, its object was to prepare men for manhood; but it seeks, on the contrary, to keep them in perpetual childhood: it is well content that the people should rejoice, provided they think of nothing but rejoicing. For their happiness such a government willingly labours, but it chooses to be the sole agent and the only arbiter of that happiness; it provides for their security, foresees and supplies their necessities, facilitates their pleasures, manages their principal concerns, directs their industry, regulates the descent of property, and subdivides their inheritances...

The result, he warned, would be that every day such government would render 'the exercise of the free agency of man less useful and less frequent'. By circumscribing the will within a narrower range it would gradually rob a man of 'all the uses of himself'.[27]

We can see now that the welfare state has had just this effect on human character. As Michael Novak has written, for more than a century socialism has 'misled the human imagination by riveting attention on the state', thus channelling humankind's social nature into the state, thereby suppressing personal responsibility and inventiveness. To avoid further decline Novak urges that we redesign our public welfare systems 'to draw forth from individual persons, their families and their associations their best (most inventive, most creative) efforts'. The post-war welfare state has permitted the human agent and civil society 'too little space for the free exercise of personal responsibility and social invention'.[28]

The policies that might follow from this approach fall into three groups: (1) policies aimed at economic growth; (2) the removal of public-policy obstacles to family or personal advancement, particularly high taxes; and (3) a focus on personal independence.

1. Economic Growth

The focus on individual conduct and morals is indispensable to success, but on its own will not be sufficient. Economic growth is a necessary, but not a sufficient, pre-condition for the creation of opportunities to escape from poverty. Economic growth depends in large measure on the energy and ingenuity of private citizens, but unwise fiscal and monetary policies can all too easily cancel out human endeavour. Government, therefore, has a responsibility to create an economic framework consistent with liberty.

2. Removal of Public-Policy Impediments

Some public policies, directly or indirectly, narrow opportunities to escape from poverty. Particular culprits are high taxes on incomes and savings, and the inadequate integration of taxes and benefits. A comprehensive reform programme is necessary to remove the impediments which make it more difficult for the poor to advance by their own endeavours. All current taxes, benefits, regulations, laws and relevant public policies, and all proposals to reform them, should be subject to 'independence impact assessments' to gauge their effect on efforts by individuals to escape from poverty by their own endeavours.

These assessments should include examination of impediments to labour mobility, such as restrictive council-house letting rules, the severe decline in the private rental sector due to rent control and other regulations which deter people from letting their property, and mortgage interest relief subsidies which tend to increase house prices, thus putting home ownership beyond the reach of the less-well paid.

Taxation policy should be subject to especially close scrutiny. Tax thresholds should be raised to allow workers to keep more of their earnings. Child tax allowances should be restored and the married person's allowance increased substantially as part of a general raising of tax thresholds and in order to bolster the traditional two-parent family. The mutual support of the family still remains the best foundation for independence.

Taxation of interest on savings has an especially harmful effect on those who want to improve their conditions by saving from earnings.

If all taxation of savings can not be abolished in the short run, the immediate introduction of a tax-free allowance of about £5,000 a year not dissimilar to the capital gains tax allowance would be feasible. Since the capital gains tax allowance already exists, but is unused by the great majority of people, it might be appropriate to redesignate it a dual 'capital gains or interest allowance', in order to benefit everyone and not only the minority who make capital gains.

3. Personal Independence Planning

There are many reasons for unemployment. Some unemployment is seasonal, some is due to the trade cycle, and some due to long-term structural changes in economic conditions. The decline of the coal industry, as coal has been replaced by other forms of energy, is an obvious example of structural unemployment. Governments can make unemployment much worse by their actions, either by failing adequately to control inflation, or by over-doing it, as in 1925 by going back on the gold standard at pre-war parities, and more recently by tying the pound to the deutschmark in the Exchange Rate Mechanism.

Here, I am concerned about people who are unemployed because they lack the skills and motivation to help themselves out of their predicament. We are not succeeding in helping this group and there is a need for new policies aimed at assisting such individuals. Focusing on individually-tailored help and advice is highly desirable but, as Mill warned, it seems unlikely that a government department can ever be the best instrument for such work. An alternative approach would be to transfer programmes intended to help particular individuals back into the workforce to private care associations, which would be charged with devising an 'independence plan' for each person.

Since April 1993, people who have been unemployed for twelve months have been required to undergo a Restart interview. At this stage they could in future be divided into two categories, those suitable for referral to an independence counselling agency and those not.

How would the scheme be paid for? One approach would be to finance the private agencies by means of a 50/50 public/private matching arrangement, that is for every pound of private money raised the government would contribute one pound up to an agreed ceiling. The agencies could also be financed by fees paid in return for finding work for their clients. For instance, they could be offered a grant of 90 per cent of the cost of income support for a twelve-month period if they found work for a client for a stipulated minimum period. This would provide a framework which would enable private associations to develop new services.

One example of a successful scheme of this type already exists in America. It is called 'America Works'. New York State places about 300 welfare recipients a year with America Works. The agency receives no fee from the State until it has found a permanent, full-time job for each beneficiary which he or she has retained for seven months. Then it receives a fee of about $5,700 dollars, significantly less than the $23,000 it costs the state in New York to keep a family of three for a year. The skill of the agency lies in persuading employers to take welfare recipients for a four-month trial period, during which America Works gives personal support in return for a fee from the employer. Usually employers pay America Works about $7.00 an hour, of which the employee gets $3.75 plus benefits. The average of $7.00 is usually about $1.00 per hour less than the going hourly rate, in recognition of the risk that employers are taking with employees who have a long record of unreliability and few skills. The employees start on a low wage but they get a chance to train and demonstrate their value to the employer, which can lead to further training or promotion.

After the four-month trial period about 70 per cent of those placed are given full-time employment at normal rates of pay; and of these, after one year 90 per cent remain in work. The key to the success of America Works is that it focuses on the personal skills of its clients. Sometimes they are given the skills to overcome discrimination, sometimes they lack self-esteem, or have little or no knowledge of how to behave in a workplace, or do not know how to seek a job interview or conduct themselves during interview, and sometimes they have been out of work for so long no employer is willing to trust them. The agency employs counsellors to improve the human capital of clients offering them coping techniques as well as workplace skills and it employs field workers to recruit employers willing to take risks.[29]

America Works illustrates the type of approach that is necessary. The focus is on personal skills and the rebuilding of character. We need to know more about the inner resources necessary to escape from poverty, and to understand the coping strategy of people who have successfully improved their own conditions despite setbacks and adversity and to discover the extent to which such skills or personal dispositions can be taught. Success stories are, in addition, both excellent teaching tools and sources of inspiration.

The 'America Works' approach means starting out on low pay, but the people who take the risk frequently end by enjoying inner satisfactions as well as material advancement. They can feel themselves beginning to live a life of reflection and choice, of mutual regard for others, and with new opportunities to contribute positively to human progress.

Conclusion

We have come through a long period during which the battle of ideas has been fought between two rival economic systems. The market economic system won the argument because it facilitated economic growth. But if communism had been capable of generating still greater growth, would that have been a decisive argument in its favour? Few think it would, yet much political debate occurs within a framework of economic rationalism. The battle against collectivist economics has led us to over-estimate the importance of markets in maintaining liberty and to neglect both the moral dimension of a free society and the corruption of law making by politics.

Civic capitalists, therefore, hope for three main changes. First, they advocate constitutional reform to re-establish the impartiality of law by separating the process of law making from the implementation of political programmes. Law making has become the politicised instrument of the majority in Parliament, but if law is to command respect it should be based on a more exacting test than a bare majority of MPs on a three-line whip.

Second, we must refresh our understanding of the moral case against the welfare state. Much of what we call the welfare state should be returned to civil society, especially education and health care, not to save money, nor to improve the 'targeting' of benefits, and not even to improve efficiency, but above all to prevent the suppression of opportunities for bringing out the best in people through service of others. The state should maintain a safety net below which no one should fall, but any help beyond the state minimum should be primarily private in order to widen the scope for individual generosity and service of others. Where services are properly a matter

152

for government, accountability should be increased through de-centralisation to localities and the removal of central government subsidies to local authorities. The result would be to increase the local taxpayers' awareness of what they were paying for and, by reducing the scope of social experiments, to increase the chances of errors being detected and corrected before too much harm is done. The general effect of these measures would be to increase the scope for civil society, that is the realm of free choice and conscience as opposed to the realm of government command.

Third, civic capitalists hope to encourage debate about the moral climate that makes freedom possible. Above all, we need a new ethos of social solidarity which rests, not on income transfers, but on mutual consideration for others and a strong sense of personal responsibility, implying a willingness to do one's bit to maintain in good order the institutions, habits, values and dispositions fundamental to liberty. We urgently need to repair the culture of personal commitment to serving the less fortunate through mutual aid or charitable work.

I close with this challenge to opinion formers. Liberty can survive considerable neglect, but unless a significant proportion of thinking people are prepared to be custodians of the culture of liberty, its demise will not be long delayed. Social-policy intellectuals invariably see themselves as radicals questioning the status quo, but in practice as Norman Dennis' studies[30] have courageously shown, they are frequently followers of fashion, conforming to the politically-correct doctrines of the day. Once radical critics of 'the capitalist establishment', they have today become tame defenders of 'the welfare establishment', unwilling to recognise fundamental flaws or to attend to unwelcome facts. Fortunately, the vacuum has been filled by some journalists, especially columnists. But while the freedom of the press has rescued us from monolithic political correctness, the challenge to thinking people remains. Liberty is based, not on self-interest, but rather on respect for law, mutual responsibility, devotion to family and love of country, yet who among us will turn his or her back on politically-correct conformity and instead stand shoulder-to-shoulder in defence of the morals and institutions without which it is impossible to maintain the free way of life characteristic of Western civilisation?

Notes

Preface

1   London: Fontana, 1992, pp. 32-36.

2   London: Longman/IEA, 1971.

Introduction

1   Novak, M., *The New Consensus on Family and Welfare*, Washington: American Enterprise Institute, 1987, p. xvi.

2   Knight, F.H., 'The sickness of liberal society' in *Freedom and Reform*, Indianapolis: Liberty Fund, 1982, p. 463.

3   Michael Novak in *The Catholic Ethic and the Spirit of Capitalism* (New York, Free Press, 1993) calls this orientation to the common good 'social justice', a term which usually means 'distributive justice'.

4   Beveridge, Lord, *Voluntary Action*, London: Allen & Unwin, 1948, p. 92, p. 328 (trade union membership is for 1912; see below p. 42 for fuller analysis of friendly society membership); Johnson, P., *Saving and Spending: The Working Class Economy in Britain 1870-1939*, Oxford: Clarendon Press, 1985, pp. 76-7.

5   My thanks are due to Michael Novak for suggesting this term to me.

Chapter 1

1   Oakeshott, M., 'The political economy of freedom' in *Rationalism in Politics and Other Essays*, 2nd edition, Indianapolis: Liberty Press, 1991, p. 387.

2   *Ibid.*, p. 388.

3   *Ibid.*, p. 388.

4   *Ibid.*, pp. 388-89.

5   Oakeshott, M., *On Human Conduct*, Oxford: Clarendon Press, 1975, pp. 313-14.

6   *Ibid.*, p. 318.

7   *Ibid.*, p. 212.

8   *Ibid.*, p. 227.

9   *Ibid.*, p. 212.

10 Alan Macfarlane in *The Origins of English Individualism* (Oxford: Blackwell, 1978) has convincingly shown the earlier origins of individualism, but he does not argue that liberty was the ruling ethos before the seventeenth century.

11 Hill, C., *The Century of Revolution, 1603–1714*, London: Sphere, 1969, p. 38.

12   Acton, J., *The History of Freedom and Other Essays*, London: Macmillan, 1907, p. 52.

13   Locke, *An Essay Concerning Human Understanding*, (ed. H.S. Pringle-Pattison), Oxford: Oxford University Press, 1924 edn, pp. 337-38.

14   Novak, M., *The Spirit of Democratic Capitalism*, 2nd edn., London: Institute of Economic Affairs, 1991; *The Catholic Ethic and the Spirit of Capitalism*. New York: Free Press, 1993.

15   For an excellent discussion of the differences between classical liberalism and libertarianism see Barry, N., *On Classical Liberalism and Libertarianism*, London: MacMillan, 1986.

16   Ricardo's main work was *Principles of Political Economy and Taxation*, 1817.

17   Hume, D., *The History of England*, 1778 edition, Indianapolis: Liberty Classics, 1983, vol. V, pp. 42-43.

18   Burke, E., *The Works of Edmund Burke*, 6 vols, London: Oxford University Press/The World's Classics, 1907, vol. 4, p. 187.

19   Smith, A., *The Wealth of Nations*, Liberty Classics edn, Indianapolis: Liberty Fund, 1981, vol. I, p. 345.

20   Marshall, A., 'Social possibilities of economic chivalry', in Pigou, A.C. (ed.) *Memorials of Alfred Marshall*, New York: Kelley and Millman, 1956, p. 343.

21   Oakeshott, *On Human Conduct*, p. 317.

22   *Loc. cit.*

23   Macaulay, T.B., *History of England*, 4 vols, London: Heron Books, 1967 edn., vol. 1, pp. 229-30.

24   Spencer, H., 'The proper sphere of government', in *The Man Versus the State (with six essays on government, society and freedom)*, Indianapolis: Liberty Fund, 1981, p. 187.

25   Hayek, *The Constitution of Liberty*, London: Routledge & Kegan Paul, 1960, p. 144.

26   *Ibid.*, p. 60.

27   *Ibid.*, p. 231.

Chapter 2

1   Oakeshott, *On Human Conduct*, pp. 234-35.

2   Marshall, A., 'The old generation of economists and the new' in Pigou, A.C. (ed) *Memorials of Alfred Marshall*, New York: Kelley and Millman, 1956, p. 310.

3   Hoover, K. and Plant, R., *Conservative Capitalism in Britain and the United States: A Critical Appraisal*, London: Routledge, 1989, p. 51. Emphasis added.

4   *Ibid.*, p. 232.

5   Ted Honderich, *Conservatism*, London: Hamish Hamilton, 1990, p. 102.

6   *Ibid.*, p. 239.

7   Tocqueville, Alexis de, *Democracy in America*, New York: Vintage Books, 1990, vol. 2, p. 121.

8   *Ibid.*, vol. 2, pp. 121-22.

9   *Ibid.*, vol. 2, p. 127.

10   *Ibid.*, vol. 1, p. 250.

11   Smith, A., *The Theory of Moral Sentiments*, Indianapolis: Liberty Fund, 1976, p. 167.

12   *Ibid.*, p. 269.

13   *Ibid.*, pp. 71-72.

14   Acton, J., *Essays in the Study and Writing of History*, Indianapolis: Liberty Fund, 1986, p. 516.

15   Novak, M., *Free Persons and the Common Good*, New York: Madison, 1989, p. 85.

16   For one of the most interesting discussions of social obligation or 'social justice' in recent years see Novak, M., *The Catholic Ethic and the Spirit of Capitalism*, New York: Free Press, 1993.

Chapter 3

1   For a comparison with the Australian friendly societies see Green, D.G. and Cromwell, L., *Mutual Aid or Welfare State*, Sydney: Allen & Unwin, 1984.

2   33 Geo. III, c.54, s.I.

3   Gosden, P.H.J.H., *The Friendly Societies in England 1815-1875*, Manchester: Manchester University Press, 1961, pp. 4-5.

4   Gosden, *Self-Help*, London: Batsford, 1973, p. 91; Beveridge, *Voluntary Action*, p. 328.

5   Gosden, *The Friendly Societies in England*, p. 18.

6   Ancient Order of Foresters, *General Laws*, Observations on the Advantages of Forestry, 1857.

7   Baernreither, J.M., *English Associations of Working Men*, London: Swan Sonnenschein, 1893, p. 380; Langridge, G.D., *A Lecture on the Origin, Rise and Progress of the Manchester Unity Independent Order of Odd Fellows*, Melbourne: Manchester Unity, 1867, pp. 20-21.

8   Webb, S. and B., *Industrial Democracy*, London: The Authors, 1913, p. 36, note 1.

9   Grand United Order of Odd Fellows, *Initiation Ceremony*, 1865, pp. 42-43.

10   Ancient Order of Foresters, *Rules*, 1907, Rule 27.

11   Ancient Order of Foresters, Lecture 1, 1879, pp. 41-42.

12   Ancient Order of Foresters, Court *Robert Gordon*, Rules 53 and 55, 1877.

13   Ancient Order of Foresters, *Formularies*, 1879, p. 12.

14   Grand United Order of Oddfellows, *Noble Grand's Charge*, 1865, pp. 23-25.

15   Ancient Order of Foresters, *General Laws*, 1857, Rule 82.

16   Ancient Order of Foresters, *General Laws*, 1857, Rule 81.

17   Independent Order of Oddfellows, Manchester Unity, *Lodge Ritual and Lecture Book with Procedure*, 1976, pp. 9-10.

18   Beveridge, *Voluntary Action*, Table 20.

19   *Ibid.*, Table 22.

20   *Ibid.*, p. 21.

21   *Ibid.*, p. 44.

22   *Ibid.*, pp. 45-50.

23   *Ibid.*, pp. 41-42.

24   *Ibid.*, pp. 58-60.

Chapter 4

1   Independent Order of Oddfellows, Manchester Unity, *Lodge Ritual and Lectures*, 1975.

2   *The Foresters Directory*, 1933, pp. xi-xii.

3   Ancient Order of Foresters, *Ceremony of Initiation*, 1879, pp. 22-23.

4   *Ritual of the Grand United Independent Order of Oddfellows*, 1865, p. 41.

5   Ancient Order of Foresters, *General Laws*, 1857, Observations on the Advantages of Forestry.

6   Ancient Order of Foresters, Lecture 3, 1879, pp. 50-51.

7   Independent Order of Oddfellows, Manchester Unity, First Degree, pp. 63-64.

8   Ancient Order of Foresters, Lecture 5, 1879, pp. 56 and 59.

9   Gosden, *The Friendly Societies in England*, pp. 5-6.

10   *Ibid.*, p. 6.

11   *Oddfellows Magazine*, July 1909, pp. 235-36.

12   Ancient Order of Foresters, Lecture 6, 1879, pp. 60-62.

Chapter 5

1   *Rules*, 1907.

2   Ancient Order of Foresters, *General Laws*, 1907, Rule 29.

3   Court *Harrison*, Ancient Order of Foresters, South Shields, *Special Court Rules*, 1915; Court *Old Abbey*, 1877, *Rules*, Rule 36.

4   Court *Robert Gordon*, Rule 42.

5   Routh, G., *Occupation and Pay in Great Britain 1906-79*, 2nd edn., London: Macmillan, 1980, pp. 100, 106, 113.

6   Rule 41, 1907.

7   Appendix A.

8   1877, Rule 14.

9   Ancient Order of Foresters, *General Laws*, 1857, Rule 36.

10 Wilkinson, J.F., *The Friendly Society Movement*, London: Longman, 1891, p. 193; Webb, S. and B., *Industrial Democracy*, p. 101, note 1.

11 *The Lancet*, 17 September 1887, p. 599; *Oddfellows Magazine*, 22 September 1889, p. 524; June 1895, pp. 187-88.

12 *Rules*, 1907, Appendix B.

13 Royal Commission on the Aged Poor, *Report*, para. 219.

14 See e.g. the *Special Rules* of Court *North Biddick*, which met in Washington, County Durham.

15 Ancient Order of Foresters, *General Laws*, 1907, Rule 71.

16 Ancient Order of Foresters, *General Laws*, 1857, Rules 92-93.

17 W.G. Cooper, *The Ancient Order of Foresters 150 Years, 1834-1984*, Southampton: AOF, 1984, pp. 14-15.

18 Siddall, T.W., *Story of a Century*, Sheffield: Independent Order of Oddfellows, Manchester Unity, Sheffield District, 1924, p. 10.

19 Independent Order of Oddfellows, Manchester Unity, New South Wales, Sydney District, *Quarterly Report*, 1856, p. 8.

20 Gosden, *The Friendly Societies in England*, p. 76.

21 Evidence of the Chief Registrar to the Royal Commission on Labour, 1892, Appendix LIII, quoted in Gosden, *The Friendly Societies in England*, Appendix A.

22 Ancient Order of Foresters, Court *Old Abbey*, *Rules*, 1877, Rule 29.

23 Ancient Order of Foresters, Court *Old Abbey*, *Laws*, 1857, Rule XXXVI.

24 Rule 29, Section 19.

25 See e.g. Ancient Order of Foresters, *General Laws*, 1907, Rule 53.

Chapter 6

1   Ancient Order of Foresters, *General Laws*, 1857, Rule 65.

2   1907, Rule 38.

3   Ancient Order of Foresters, *General Laws*, 1907, Rule 38.

4   Langridge, G.D., *A Lecture on the Origin, Rise and Progress of the Manchester Unity Independent Order of Odd Fellows*, Melbourne: Manchester Unity, 1867, pp. 20-21; see also Wilkinson, J.F., *The Friendly Society Movement*, London: Longman, 1891, p. 204.

5   *General Laws*, 1857, Rule 66.

6   Royal Commission on the Poor Laws, 1909, Appendix V, Q. 52127.

7   Royal Commission on Labour, 1893, Fourth Report, Minutes of Evidence (sitting as a whole), Qs. 1331-32.

8   Royal Commission on the Aged Poor, 1895, Q. 11039.

9   Royal Commission on the Poor Laws, 1909, Appendix III, Qs. 35147(7), 35174-80.

10 *Ibid.*, Appendix III, Q. 35147(10).

11 Royal Commission on the Poor Laws, Appendix XIV, pp. 106, 134, 157.

12 Beveridge, *Voluntary Action*, p. 76.

13 Rowntree, B.S., *Poverty: A Study of Town Life*, London: Macmillan, 1901, p. 357n.; emphasis in original.

14 Gilbert, B.B., *The Evolution of National Insurance in Great Britain*, London: Michael Joseph, 1966, pp. 166-67.

15 *Oddfellows Magazine*, February 1898, pp. 40-46; April 1901, pp. 103-4.

16 Royal Commission on the Poor Laws, 1909, Appendix IV, Qs. 37377-84.

17 *Ibid.*, Appendix IV, Qs. 41792-800.

18 *Ibid.*, Appendix IV, Appendix LII (2).

19 *Ibid.*, Appendix XIV, pp. 106-7.

20 *Ibid.*, Appendix XIV, p. 107.

21 *Ibid.*, Appendix XIV, p. 157.

22 *Ibid.*, Appendix VII, Qs. 77557-58.

23 *Ibid.*, Appendix VII, Qs. 77543-44.

24 Select Committee on the Aged Deserving Poor, 1899, Qs. 1701-2.

25 Royal Commission on the Poor Laws, 1909, Appendix IV, Q. 41804; Appendix VII, Q. 77538.

26 Royal Commission on the Aged Poor, 1895, Qs. 11236-37.

27 Royal Commission on the Poor Laws, 1909, Appendix IV, Qs. 43219-20; see also *BMJ Supplement*, 22 July 1905, p. 7.

Chapter 7

1   See Green, D.G., *Working Class Patients and the Medical Establishment*, Aldershot: Gower, 1985, for an extended account of the friendly societies' battle with the medical profession. (This book is now out of print, but a few copies are still available from the IEA.)

2   Royal Commission on the Poor Laws, 1909, *Report*, p. 259.

3   *Ibid.*, Appendix IV, Q. 38390.

4   22 July 1853, p. 652.

5   *Whitaker's Almanack*, 1900, p. 411; McConaghey, R.M.S., 'Medical practice in the days of Mackenzie', *The Practitioner*, vol. 196, 1966, p. 155; Peterson, M.J., *The Medical Profession in Mid-Victorian London*, Berkeley: University of California Press, 1978, pp. 211-13.

6   *Oddfellows Magazine*, June 1889, p. 177.

7   *Oddfellows Magazine*, August 1909, p. 489; Cox, A., *Among the Doctors*, London: Christopher Johnson, no date shown [1950], p. 22.

8   Routh, *Occupation and Pay in Great Britain 1906-79*, pp. 100, 106, 113.

9   *BMJ Supplement*, 22 July 1905, p. 9.

10 *Report as to the Practice of Medicine and Surgery by Unqualified Persons*, 1910, Cd. 5422, London: HMSO, pp. 3-4, 8.

11 Royal Commission on the Poor Laws, 1909, Appendix V, Q. 50566.

12 *Hansard*, 1889, vol. 338, cols. 1552-55; Abel-Smith, B., *The Hospitals 1800-1948*, London: Heinemann, 1964, p. 153.

13 *British Medical Journal*, 14 September 1907, p. 658; *The Lancet*, 1 June 1907, pp. 1543-50.

14 *British Medical Journal*, 14 September, 1907, p. 658.

15 British Medical Association Medico-Political Committee, 'An investigation into the economic conditions of contract medical practice in the United Kingdom', *British Medical Journal Supplement*, 22 July 1905, pp. 1-96 (hereafter, *BMJ Supplement*, 22 July 1905).

16 *Ibid.*, p. 9.

17 Royal Commission on the Poor Laws, 1909, Appendix IV, Q. 47501.

18 *The Lancet*, 5 October 1895, p. 875.

19 *BMJ Supplement*, 22 July 1905, p. 10.

20 *Ibid.*, p. 9.

21 Royal Commission on the Poor Laws, 1909, Appendix IV, Q. 43998(43).

22 *BMJ Supplement*, 22 July 1905, pp. 21-22.

23 *BMJ Supplement*, 22 July 1905, p. 23.

24 *The Lancet*, 1849, p. 570; *Association Medical Journal*, 2 September 1853, p. 766; 7 October 1853, p. 888.

25 *The Lancet*, 1869, vol. 1, p. 60.

26 *British Medical Journal*, 10 June 1871, p. 626; 24 June 1871, p. 676.

27 3 November 1877, p. 654.

28 *British Medical Journal*, 23 October 1869, p. 449; 27 November 1869, p. 600; *The Lancet*, 11 December 1869, p. 831.

29 *Oddfellows Magazine*, October 1877, pp. 241-43.

30   *The Lancet*, 26 October 1895, pp. 1070-71.

31   *Foresters Miscellany*, April 1884, pp. 86-87.

32   *Foresters Miscellany*, April 1884, p. 89; 1886, p. 145.

33   *Foresters Directory*, 1896, pp. 593-96; *British Medical Journal*, 10 June 1899, p. 1413.

34   1966, p. 309.

35   *The Lancet*, 21 September, 1895, p. 1053.

36   *The Lancet*, 21 September 1895, p. 757.

37   *British Medical Journal*, 23 November 1895, p. 1319; *British Medical Journal*, 30 November 1895, p. 1368.

38   *British Medical Journal*, 1896, vol. 1, p. 999; vol. 2, p. 8; 1897, vol. 1, p. 168.

39   e.g. *Association Medical Journal*, 7 October 1853, p. 888.

40   *British Medical Journal*, 22 October 1892, p. 920.

41   Report of the Committee on Medical Aid Associations, General Medical Council, *Minutes*, Appendix XII, 1893, p. 8.

42   *Ibid.*, p. 18.

43   *Ibid.*, p. 24.

44   *Foresters Miscellany*, August 1893, p. 142.

45   *Oddfellows Magazine*, March 1893, p. 68.

46   *British Medical Journal*, 24 March 1900, p. 739.

47   See e.g. *British Medical Journal*, 15 June 1901, p. 1500.

48   Little, E.M., *History of the British Medical Association 1832-1932*, London: BMA, 1932, p. 205.

49   *British Medical Journal*, 6 June 1903, pp. 1339-41; BMJ, 13 June 1903, pp. 1380-81.

50   Royal Commission on the Poor Laws, 1909, Appendix VII, Q. 77408.

51   *BMJ Supplement*, 22 July 1905, pp. 12-13.

52   *Oddfellows Magazine*, April 1897, p. 99; see also February 1890, p. 48.

53   *The Lancet*, 18 February 1871, p. 239.

54   Chief Registrar of Friendly Societies, *Annual Report*, 1918; Comyns Carr, A.S., Stuart Garnett, W.H. and Taylor, J.H., *National Insurance*, 1st edn., London: Macmillan, 1912, p. 193; *Foresters Directory*, 1896; Little, E.M., *History of the British Medical Association 1832-1932*, London: BMA, 1932, p. 205.

55   *Oddfellows Magazine*, July 1909, p. 411.

56   *Foresters Miscellany*, November 1911, p. 742.

57   *Oddfellows Magazine*, July 1911, pp. 353-54.

58   *Oddfellows Magazine*, September 1910, p. 664.

59   *British Medical Journal*, 13 February 1909, p. 425.

60 *British Medical Journal*, 23 October, 1869, p. 457.

61 See *The Lancet*, 1871, vol. 2, pp. 790-91.

62 *Oddfellows Magazine*, July 1890, p. 219.

63 *British Medical Journal*, 18 January 1896, p. 172.

64 *British Medical Journal Supplement*, 28 May 1904, pp. 132-33; 22 July 1905, p. 26.

65 *British Medical Journal*, 18 June 1904, p. 1458.

66 Beveridge, *Voluntary Action*, p. 331.

Chapter 8

1   Trades Union Congress, *The Book of the Martyrs of Tolpuddle 1834-1934*, London: TUC, 1934.

2   Quoted in Gosden, *Self Help*, p. 64. (Emphasis added.)

3   Gosden, *The Friendly Societies in England 1815-1875*, p. 188; Sir Edward Brabrook later thought that about 50 per cent of English societies were unregistered, see above p. 65.

4   *Ibid.*, p. 97.

5   *Ibid.*, p. 104.

6   *Loc. cit.*

7   *Ibid.*, p. 106.

8   *Loc. cit.*

9   Gosden, *Self Help*, p. 97.

10 Gosden, *The Friendly Societies in England 1815-1875*, p. 108.

11 Beveridge, *Voluntary Action*, pp. 66-7.

12 Gosden, *Self Help*, p. 99.

Chapter 9

1   Some of the material in this chapter is taken from my earlier book *Working Class Patients and the Medical Establishment*; some from an IEA pamphlet, Green, D.G., *The Welfare State: For Rich or For Poor* (1982); and much of the material about the medical institutes and medical aid societies was tucked away as a little-noticed appendix to Green, D.G., *Which Doctor?*, also published by the IEA (1985).

2   *British Medical Journal*, 6 January 1903, p. 1339.

3   *British Medical Journal*, 12 November 1910, p. 1556.

4   See e.g. *British Medical Journal*, 4 July 1896, p. 10.

5   Gilbert, B.B., *The Evolution of National Insurance in Great Britain: The Origins of the Welfare State*, London: Michael Joseph, 1966, pp. 327-28, quoting a memorandum drafted by Lloyd George in August 1910.

6   *Ibid.*, p. 360.

7   Bunbury, Sir Henry, ed., *Lloyd George's Ambulance Wagon*, London: Methuen, 1957, p. 212.

8   Klein, R., *Complaints Against Doctors*, London: Charles Knight, 1973, p. 60.

9   *Report on the British Health Services*, London: Political and Economic Planning 1937, p. 231.

10 *Ibid*, p. 152.

11 British Medical Association, General Practice Committee, Documents 1938-39, GP107, pp. 1-6.

12 *British Medical Journal Supplement*, 10 December 1938, pp. 357-62.

13 BMA, Medico-Political Committee, Documents, 1936-37, MP31, pp. 14-18.

14 Public Records Office, PIN8/88.

15 In *Working Class Patients and the Medical Establishment*, I estimated that only three-quarters of the female members would have signed up for medical benefit, but on further investigation it seems more likely that the vast majority attended the lodge doctor.

16 *Oddfellows Magazine*, May 1925, pp. 256-57.

17 *Foresters Miscellany*, May 1923, pp. 214-15.

18 PEP, 1937, p. 154.

19 National Deposit Friendly Society, *Rules*, 1949, rules 87, 91.

20 BMA, Medico-Political Committee, Documents 1936-37, MP75.

21 Public Records Office, MH81/54.

22 BMA, General Practice Committee, Documents, 1938-39, GP107, pp. 6, 9-10.

23 *Report of Sir William Plender to the Chancellor of the Exchequer on the result of his investigation into existing conditions in respect of medical attendance and remuneration in certain towns*, Cd 6305, London: HMSO, 1912, p. 128.

24 Insurance Commission (England), *Report on the Administration in England of the National Insurance Act, 1912-13*, London: HMSO, pp. 147-48.

Chapter 10

1   Beveridge, *Social Insurance and Allied Services*, 1942, Cmd. 6404, pp. 26-27.

2   *Ibid.*, p. 31.

3 In *The Times*, 5 February 1946, reprinted in Lincoln, J.A., ed., *The Way Ahead: The Strange Case of the Friendly Societies*, London: National Conference of Friendly Societies, 1946.

4 Public Records Office, MH77/93.

5 *Ibid.*

6 *Ibid.*

7 *Ibid.*

8 *Ibid.*

9 *Ibid.*

10 Report of meeting issued by Ministry of Health, Public Records Office, MH77/94.

11 Friendly Societies Medical Alliance, *Annual Report*, 1945, in Public Records Office MH77/94.

12 *Ibid.*

13 Friendly Societies Medical Alliance, *Annual Report*, pp. 17-19, in Public Records Office MH77/94.

14 Hayek, F.A., *Law, Legislation and Liberty*, 3 vols, vol. 1, *Rules and Order*, London: Routledge & Kegan Paul, 1973, pp. 14-15.

15 PEP, 1937, p. 2.

16 *Ibid.*, p. 150 (emphasis added).

17 Public Records Office, MH77/93.

18 Public Records Office, MH77/94.

19 *Ibid.*

20 *Ibid.*

21 Emphasis added in original.

22 Public Records Office, MH77/94.

23 *Ibid.*

24 Public Records Office, MH77/95.

25 *Parliamentary Debates*, House of Commons, 1959-60, vol. 615, cols. 11-12.

26 *Parliamentary Debates*, House of Commons, 1966-67, vol. 728, col. 17.

Chapter 11

1 Mill, J.S., *On Liberty*, (with *Utilitarianism* and *On Representative Government*), Everyman edn., London: Dent, 1972, p. 238.

2 Hayek, F.A., *Law, Legislation and Liberty*, 3 vols, vol. 3, *The Political Order of a Free People*, 1979, pp. 112-13.

3   Mill, J.S., *Principles of Political Economy*, London: Longmans, 1909 edn., Book V, Chapter XI.

4   Hayek, *The Constitution of Liberty*, pp. 221-22.

5   Seldon, A., *Capitalism*, Oxford: Blackwell, 1990, pp. 10-11, pp. 169-70.

6   *Ibid.*, p. 243.

7   Hayek, F.A., *The Constitution of Liberty*, p. 223.

8   Hayek, F.A., *The Constitution of Liberty*, p. 225.

9   In addition, the poll tax was imposed on individuals rather than families, the natural units of human living, and, unlike a property-based tax, took no account of ability to pay.

10 Popper, Sir Karl, *The Open Society and Its Enemies*, 2 vols, London: Routledge & Kegan Paul, 1966.

11 Dennis, N. and Erdos, G., *Families Without Fatherhood*, London: IEA, 1992.

12 *Ibid.*

13 Wilson, J.Q., 'The family-values debate', *Commentary*, April 1993, pp. 24-31.

14 Schumpeter, J.A., *Capitalism, Socialism and Democracy*, London: George Allen & Unwin, 1976, 5th edn., p. 158.

15 Knight, F., 'Social science and the political trend', in *Freedom and Reform*, Indianapolis: Liberty Press, 1982, pp. 32-33.

16 Barry, N., 'The social market economy', *Social Philosophy and Policy*, 1993, p. 7.

17 *Ibid.*, p. 13.

18 Barry, N., 'Political and economic thought of German neo-liberals' in Peacock, A.T. and Willgerodt, H. (eds) *Neo-Liberals and the Social Market Economy*, London: Macmillan, 1989, pp. 105-24.

19 Hayek, F.A., *The Constitution of Liberty*, p. 265.

20 See Novak, M., *The Spirit of Democratic Capitalism*, London: IEA, 1991; and *The Catholic Ethic and the Spirit of Capitalism*, New York: Free Press, 1993, for an excellent discussion of this fundamental quality of capitalism.

21 *Politics, Markets and America's Schools*, Washington: Brookings Institution, 1990, p. 214.

22 Green, D.G., *Challenge to the NHS*, London: IEA, 1986.

23 Green, D.G., *Everyone a Private Patient*, London: IEA, 1988.

24 Madison J., quoted in Acton, J., *Essays in the History of Liberty*, Indianapolis: Liberty Fund, 1986, p. 220.

25 Mill, *Principles of Political Economy*, pp. 967-8.

26 *Ibid.*, p. 969.

27 Tocqueville, Alexis de, *Democracy in America*, New York: Vintage Books, 1990, vol. II, pp. 318-19.

28 Novak, M., *The Crisis of the Welfare State*, London: Centre for Policy Studies, 1993, pp. 10, 13.

29 America Works, *Prospectus*; *Newsweek*, 29 June 1992; *HR Magazine for Human Resource Management*, July 1991, vol. 36, no. 7, pp. 36-38.

30 Dennis, N. and Erdos, G., *Families Without Fatherhood*, London: IEA, 1992; Dennis, N., *Rising Crime and the Dismembered Family: How Conformist Intellectuals Have Undermined Common Sense*, London: IEA, forthcoming.